SEO Toolbook:

Free SEO tools for Google & Bing

2016 Edition

by Jason McDonald, Ph.D.

© Spring, 2016, JM Internet Group

https://www.jm-seo.org/

INTRODUCTION

Search Engine Optimization or "**SEO**," of course, is the art and science of getting your company or organization to the top of relevant searches on Google. SEO, in other words, is how smart people get **free advertising on Google**, **Bing**, or **Yahoo**.

With 85% market share, Google dominates search, and it is to Google that most customers go 24/7 to find companies, products, and services. Being on page one of Google, for free, or even better in one of the top three "organic" results on the search giant, means a free ad on Google running 24/7, a free ad appearing when potential customers search for your company, service or product. To get on Bing or Yahoo is just icing on the cake, and more free advertising.

- *What, my friend, could possibly be better than* **free advertising on Google**?

Free SEO Tools - that's what. Better than *free* advertising on Google is using *free* tools to get there in the first place. That's what *SEO Toolbook* is all about: **free** tools to help you get to the top of Google's **free** listings.

Here are my latest favorite, free tools for total Google (and Bing / Yahoo) domination via SEO, updated for Spring, 2016. **New** for this edition, I have added new **chapters**, new **informational resources** and even a list of fun-filled **Google Easter eggs**, which will totally impress you and all your computer nerd friends.

TO DO LIST:

» Understand How *SEO Toolbook* Works

» Register Your Copy Online

» Contents

» Acknowledge the Copyright and Disclaimer

» Write a Review, Get a Free eBook

» UNDERSTAND HOW *SEO TOOLBOOK* WORKS

First and foremost, *SEO Toolbook* assumes a **working knowledge of SEO**. This toolbook has many wonderful free tools, but the tools alone are useless without a knowledge of how the game is played! (If you need that knowledge, I recommend you check out my *SEO Fitness Workbook* (on Amazon at http://jmlinks.com/8c), online courses at https://www.jm-seo.org/, or call 800-298-4065 to learn more about my SEO one-on-one training and consulting services).

Second, this book emphasizes only **free** tools. Despite the fact that there are quite a few *paid* SEO tools out there, none are any better than the free tools identified in this *Toolbook*. Indeed, in today's tight economy, why pay when you can get them for free? Not to mention, why pay when the most important element, i.e. a knowledge of how SEO is played to win, can't be obtained from any tool?

Third, I have reviewed each tool in the *Toolbook* for relevance and ease of use. Almost without exception, the tools in the *Toolbook* require nothing more than a Web browser and active connection to the Internet. *Easy* is just as important as *free*. Generally speaking, if a tool requires registration or has only a "trial" period, it has been excluded.

» REGISTER YOUR COPY ONLINE

If you've purchased this *Toolbook* in hard copy format, be aware that if you register online, you get instant access to a PDF copy, which has easy, clickable links to all resources. To do so, simply:

- Go to http://jmlinks.com/8d.
- Sign up as indicated.
- You'll be transferred to my "SEO Dashboard"
  - There, you'll have easy access to the BEST tools as identified herein.
  - You can also download a PDF copy of this *Toolbook* which can be read online and will have clickable links.

Note: *if you email me your Amazon receipt, I will rebate you 50% of your cost once you sign up for the email alert system.*

» CONTENTS

The *Toolbook* follows the steps to effective SEO that I teach in my *SEO Fitness Workbook*, online classes, and contains the following categories of tools:

1. **FAQs** – tutorials and "frequently asked questions" documents on SEO
2. **Keywords** - tools to identify and measure your keywords
3. **Page Tags** - tools to help analyze your on page HTML tags
4. **Link Building and Social Mentions** - tools to identify link and social media targets
5. **Content Marketing** – tools and tips for building a content-marketing system to feed your website (and social media) with fresh content
6. **Blogs and Blogging** - tools to help you be a better blogger as well as identify bloggers who might help you with links or social mentions
7. **Press Releases** - services to publish your news, for free, on the Internet
8. **Rank** - tools to measure your rank on Google searches
9. **Diagnostics** – tools to "diagnosis" the health of your website as well as conduct SEO checkups
10. **Website Structure** - tools to create the most effective SEO website structure
11. **Local Search** - tools to help get your company to the top of Google+ local and local searches
12. **Google+** - information and tools about Google's social media network, Google+, which can help you tremendously with your SEO performance
13. **Google** – a cornucopia of all the free resources and tools provided by Google
14. **Metrics** - tools to help you measure (and understand) your inbound web traffic
15. **Media** - the top blogs and resources to stay up-to-date on SEO
16. **Shows & Conferences** – the top conferences on search engine optimization
17. **Easter Eggs** – humorous hidden treasures inside the Google search engine, wonderfully designed to waste time and impress your (nerd) friends

Get More Free Stuff!

You can find out about my other toolbooks, workbooks, and free resources by signing up for my email alerts at https://jm-seo.org/free.

Finally, the *Toolbook* is really mean to be read "online" rather than "on paper," since all of the links are clickable. As you read about an interesting tools, I encourage to click over and check each tool out. SEO is a learn-by-doing art, and so are the tools!

Let's get started!

▶▶ ACKNOWLEDGE THE COPYRIGHT AND DISCLAIMER

▶▶ WRITE A REVIEW, GET MORE FREE STUFF

Reviews on Amazon really help me spread the word about free SEO and free SEO tools. If you are inclined, write an honest review of this book on Amazon. Then, email me that your review is up. I'll "gift" you a copy of one of my other books, such as my *SEO Fitness*

Workbook or *Social Media Marketing Workbook*. Offer is limited to the first consecutive twenty reviewers.

» MEET THE AUTHOR

My name is Jason McDonald, and I have been active on the Internet since 1994 (*having invented the Internet along with Al Gore*) and taught SEO, AdWords, and Social Media since 2009 – online, at Stanford University Continuing Studies, at both AcademyX and the Bay Area Video Coalition in San Francisco, at workshops, and in corporate trainings across these United States. I love figuring out how things work, and I love teaching others! SEO is an endeavor that I understand, and I want to empower you to understand it as well.

Learn more about me at https://www.jasonmcdonald.org/ or at my corporate website https://www.jm-seo.org/. Or just call 800-298-4065, say something flattering, and I my secretary will put you through. *(Like I have a secretary! Just call if you have something to ask or say).*

1

FAQs

You got questions? They got answers. I, of course, recommend that you either purchase my companion *SEO Fitness Workbook* on Amazon (http://jmlinks.com/8c), or sign up for my paid classes at https://www.jm-seo.org/. But recognizing the importance of free, here are my favorite free "Frequently Asked Questions" documents and tutorials on SEO. Never stop learning!

GOOGLE SEO STARTER GUIDE - http://bit.ly/google-seo-starter

This is the one, and only, really good resource by Google that is an official guide to what to do when, how, where and why for SEO. It covers mainly 'on page' SEO but definitely identifies basic tasks to accomplish on your website. Highly recommended.

Rating: 5 Stars | **Category:** resource

SEARCH ENGINE LAND'S GUIDE TO SEO - http://searchengineland.com/guide/seo

Search Engine Land is clearly the top blog on search engine optimization. They provide this in-depth and pretty useful guide to SEO for their readership. They have a periodic table of SEO factors, which is a completely bizarre way to explain factors that have different ranks. But, oh well, they failed chemistry in High School but paid attention in math. This guide is a useful, basic guide to the subject.

Rating: 4 Stars | **Category:** tutorial

SEO FOR WORDPRESS - https://yoast.com/wordpress-seo/

This guide is by the YOAST folks, who produce the most popular plugins for SEO and WordPress. It is very, very technical and as such completely overemphasizes the technical side of SEO to the huge detriment of the marketing / content marketing side of the equation. So it shows its age and its old, traditional perspective on the subject. But it is a useful checklist of technical things to do in WordPress, for sure.

Rating: 3 Stars | **Category:** resource

MOZ SEO BEGINNERS GUIDE - https://moz.com/beginners-guide-to-seo

MOZ is one of the top providers of (paid) SEO tools. It provides this basic introductory tutorial to SEO. Aimed at beginners, and (over)emphasizes technical SEO. But, hey, it's free.

Rating: 3 Stars | **Category:** tutorial

QUICKSPROUT SEO GUIDE - http://www.quicksprout.com/the-advanced-guide-to-seo/

Billed as an 'Advanced' guide, this is really more of a basic or beginner's look at SEO. Like the MOZ guide, it overemphasizes technical SEO and underemphasizes content marketing.

Rating: 3 Stars | **Category:** tutorial

HOW GOOGLE SEARCH WORKS - http://www.google.com/insidesearch/howsearchworks/thestory/

Have you ever wondered how Google works? This somewhat cheeky guide is by Google about Google. It's a beginner's guide to how Google crawls the Web, and how it ranks the results on the Google search response page. Beginner level, but the basics of SEO are incredibly important!

Rating: 3 Stars | **Category:** overview

SEO - SEARCH ENGINE OPTIMIZATION WIKIPEDIA ENTRY - http://en.wikipedia.org/wiki/Search_engine_optimization

Wikipedia - the free online encyclopedia - has a great starting point to SEO and SEO topics. It begins: "Search engine optimization (SEO) as a subset of search engine marketing seeks to improve the number and quality of visitors to a web site from 'natural' ('organic' or 'algorithmic') search results."

Rating: 3 Stars | **Category:** overview

GOOGLE SEO CHEAT SHEET - http://googlewebmastercentral.blogspot.com/2013/03/cheat-sheet-for-friends-and-family.html

This Google Webmaster Here is Google's one page SEO cheat sheet. This is a VERY basic guide to SEO, especially on page. Note: it's a PDF file but sometimes it doesn't show up like that when you download it. So you may have to "tell" your PC / MAC that it's a PDF file.

Rating: 2 Stars | **Category:** book

2

KEYWORDS

Keywords are fundamental to SEO. Your customers start their quest to "find you" by typing in **keywords** or **keyphrases** into Google, Yahoo, or Bing. Therefore, identifying and organizing **customer-centric keywords** is the foundation of effective SEO. Your best keywords match your **unique value proposition** with **high volume keywords** used by your customers. Think **volume** plus **value** as you chart out your keyword worksheet.

Here are the best **free** SEO keyword tools on the Internet, ranked with the best tools first!

GOOGLE KEYWORD PLANNER - https://adwords.google.com/KeywordPlanner

This is Google's keyword planner. It has now become the primary Google-based tool for keyword research. Be sure to watch Jason's YouTube video on how to use it, as the user interface leaves much to be desired! Still, it is the best tool for researching keyword volume vs. value (CPC) data.

Rating: 5 Stars | **Category:** tool

UBERSUGGEST - http://ubersuggest.org

Do you love Google suggest (the drop-down suggestions displayed when you type into Google)? It's great for keyword discovery. Ubersuggest is even better - it does a variety of things to provide all sorts of keyword suggestions. So it's a wonderful keyword discovery tool!

Rating: 5 Stars | **Category:** tool

SPYFU - http://spyfu.com

SpyFu will track your ads and competitors ads. Similar to KeywordSpy but not as good. Nonetheless, input a competitor's domain and you can see their ads and some basic information on their keywords and bids.

Rating: 5 Stars | **Category:** tool

BING WEBMASTER TOOLS - http://bing.com/toolbox/webmaster

Interested in Bing? This is the Bing Webmaster Tools home page. Similar to the Google suite. Has some new features that are radically improving this tool from Bing. Includes a good keyword discovery tool.

Rating: 5 Stars | **Category:** tool

KEYWORDSPY - http://keywordspy.com

KeywordSpy currently operates in USA, United Kingdom, Australia and Canada. Through this keyword tool and keyword software, you can perform advanced keyword research and keyword tracking to study what your competitors have been advertising in their AdWords campaigns and other PPC campaigns. You can get complete in-depth analysis, stats, budget, affiliates & ad copies of your competitors.

Rating: 5 Stars | **Category:** tool

RELATED KEYWORDS - http://pagerank.net/related-keywords

Related Keywords enables you to identify related keywords and search terms that are closely related for your SEO optimization efforts. One of the FEW tools that's good for finding synonyms: lawyer vs. attorney, class vs. course, etc.

Rating: 5 Stars | **Category:** tool

SERPSTAT - http://sg.serpstat.com

Yet another amazing and fun tool based on Google suggest / suggested searches. Enter your keyword and brainstorm keyword ideas. Allows you to select Google top level domain (e.g., google.com, google.co.uk) for non-US search suggestions.

Rating: 5 Stars | **Category:** tool

GOOGLE GLOBAL MARKET FINDER - http://translate.google.com/globalmarketfinder

This is a new and different spin on the Google keywords tool. You can use it to browse keyword trends by countries, and you can drill down into synonyms based on the primary Google keyword tool. In some ways it's just a cooler, faster way to generate a list of keyword synonyms even if you aren't really interested in geography. Check it out, it's a COOL TOOL.

Rating: 5 Stars | **Category:** tool

GOOGLE SUGGEST AND GOOGLE RELATED SEARCHES - http://google.com

From the Google home page, enter a target keyword phrase such as 'flower shop'. First, notice the keywords 'suggested' in the drop-down list - this is called Google Suggest, and can be very useful. Second, do an actual search, then scroll down to the VERY bottom, and look for 'Searches related to flower shop' to see searches related to your search term. Fantastic ways to identify potential target keywords and key phrases!

Rating: 4 Stars | **Category:** tool

iSpionage - http://ispionage.com

iSpionage is an amazingly cool tool that allows you to take a keyword or a website, and reverse engineer all variations of that keyword. Great for keyword research - especially keyword discovery. Free variant is pretty powerful!

Rating: 4 Stars | **Category:** tool

SEOCentro Keyword Density Tool - http://seocentro.com/tools/seo/keyword-density.html

One element critical to SEO success is having good keyword density. A page that has good keyword density - such as three to seven percent of content - will outrank a page with lower density, all things considered. However, you also don't want to go overboard and have too many keywords. Input a web URL into this tool and it generates a cool 'keyword cloud' as well as helping you see the density.

Rating: 4 Stars | **Category:** tool

Soovle - http://soovle.com

Let the web help - generate your keywords, that is. Type a keyword or phrase that interests you for SEO into Soovle and this nifty tool will generate phrase upon phrase of helper keywords. Very useful for idea generation and blogging.

Rating: 4 Stars | **Category:** tool

Thesaurus.com - http://thesaurus.com

Thesaurus.com takes the concept of the old paper thesaurus and puts it online. Enter a search term such as, 'lawyer,' and find relevant synonyms and keyword ideas such as 'attorney,' 'barrister,' 'law firm,' etc. Great for keyword discovery!

Rating: 4 Stars | **Category:** tool

KEYWORD DENSITY CHECKER - KEYWORD CLOUD - http://webconfs.com/keyword-density-checker.php

> This tool provides two perspectives on keyword density. Enter a URL and this tool will create a Keyword Cloud and provide a Keyword Density listing. A Keyword Cloud is a visual depiction of keywords used on a website. Keywords having higher density are depicted in a larger fonts. Ideally your main keywords should appear in larger fonts at the start of the cloud. The Keyword Density listing is a list of all keywords on the page ordered by count and density percentage. You can also pop a competitor in here to get keyword ideas!
>
> **Rating:** 4 Stars | **Category:** tool

KEYWORD TOOL - https://serps.com/tools/keywords

> Input your keyword or a keyword phrase, and this nifty - new - tool gives you many of the related phrases. Of note: it gives you volume and value information, which is better than many of these 'suggest' type of tools.
>
> **Rating:** 4 Stars | **Category:** tool

KEYWORD NICHE FINDER - http://wordstream.com/keyword-niche-finder

> Really this tool is about finding related keywords. Enter a target keyword and the tool will generate a list of closely related keywords. Then click on any one of those, and the right hand side of the screen will show clusters of those related tools. It is a good tool for keyword discovery, not unlike Google's Wonder Wheel or related searches.
>
> **Rating:** 4 Stars | **Category:** tool

SEM RUSH - http://www.semrush.com/

> Similar to KeywordSpy, this tool allows you to enter a domain or a competitor, and returns a list of AdWords keywords they are running under as well as their organic keywords. Use it to track a competitor, as well as to generate a keyword list (keyword discovery).

Rating: 4 Stars | **Category:** tool

SEO BOOK KEYWORD TOOL - http://tools.seobook.com/keyword-tools/seobook

SEO Book produces this free keyword research / suggestion tool. Useful to help you think of a good keyword / key phrase list. You must sign up for a free account, but then you can access a good list of keywords. Very similar to the paid tool, Wordtracker, but free - so how can you complain?

Rating: 4 Stars | **Category:** tool

CONTENT FOREST - KEYWORDKIWI - http://www.contentforest.com/keywordkiwi

Don't understand the name - is this a play on the infamous 'Kiwi fruit' of New Zealand? No matter, this is a great tool for finding keyword phrases. Enter a keyword, and like Ubersuggest, it gives you a list of related keywords.

Rating: 3 Stars | **Category:** tool

KEYWORD FINDER - https://kwfinder.com

A very fun, interesting tool to discover keywords.

Rating: 3 Stars | **Category:** tool

HIGH PAYING KEYWORDS - http://www.pagerank.net/high-paying-keywords

This tool helps identify highest CPC (Cost Per Click) keywords / keyword phrases (i.e., search terms) advertisers are bidding on. This enables you as a website owner/marketer to understand the most valuable keywords, both for Google AdWords campaigns and/or organic SEO efforts.

Rating: 3 Stars | **Category:** tool

TAGCROWD - http://tagcrowd.com

Input your website URL or any URL, and this nifty program will create a tag cloud of keywords density on your site. It's a useful self-check for keywords / keyword density.

Rating: 3 Stars | **Category:** tool

KEYWORD SUGGESTION - http://pagerank.net/keyword-suggestion

Yet another tool for keyword discovery. Enter a 'starter' keyword and get suggestions based on volume and value.

Rating: 3 Stars | **Category:** tool

SEOCentro KEYWORD SUGGESTION TOOL - http://seocentro.com/tools/search-engines/keyword-suggestion.html

Enter a keyword and it polls Google, Bing, and Yahoo to consolidate their suggestions. Great for keyword discovery as it will suggest close, or related keyword terms.

Rating: 3 Stars | **Category:** tool

ALEXA - http://www.alexa.com/

Alexa is (yet another) search engine. One of its unique features is site statistics and traffic information for each returned item. You can use it, therefore, to 'reverse engineer' competitors. It also provides some inbound link data and keyword data for those competitors - so useful for link building research and competitive keyword research.

Rating: 3 Stars | **Category:** engine

FREE NEGATIVE KEYWORD TOOL - http://wordstream.com/negative-keywords

Enter your core keyword and this tool gives you 'food for thought' in terms of possible negative keywords. Negative keywords are critical for AdWords, since you pay per click - use this tool to help you find words you DO NOT WANT.

Rating: 3 Stars | **Category:** tool

WORDLE CREATE WORD CLOUDS - http://wordle.net/create

This tool takes a little tweaking but is very interesting. First, take a competitors page. Second, do a COPY ALL / CTRL+A in FireFox and copy all the text on the page. Second, paste this content into the text box and hit GO. Third, look at the resulting 'word cloud' - the bigger words are more prominent, and ultimately more powerful to Google.

Rating: 3 Stars | **Category:** tool

KEYWORD TOOL - http://keywordtool.io

Similar to Ubersuggest, this tool builds upon Google Suggest to provide a list of 'helper' words and phrases. For example, enter insoles and you'll see shoe insoles, insoles for runners, etc. It also provides questions containing the keyword users enter when searching Google and keyword suggestions for YouTube, Bing and Apple App Store. Great for finding helper words as part of keyword research. Additional related data like keyword search volume and CPC requires paid account.

Rating: 3 Stars | **Category:** tool

BRUCE CLAY'S SEOTOOLSET TOOLS - http://seotoolset.com/tools/free_tools.html

Bruce Clay is a guru in Search Engine Optimization. Use this page to access many of his free tools. The best are: Single Page Analyzer, Link Analysis Report, Keyword Suggestion Tool. Useful primarily for keyword discovery and checking your page tags vs. target keywords.

Rating: 2 Stars | **Category:** tool

SEARCH TERM SUGGESTION / KEYWORD DISCOVERY TOOL - http://keyworddiscovery.com/search.html

Free trial of the Trellian keyword discovery tool. Enter a keyword and it finds many synonyms and phrases. Great so you don't miss out on the soda / pop, sneaker / tennis shoes, attorney / lawyer synonyms.

Rating: 2 Stars | **Category:** tool

GOOGLE NGRAM VIEWER - http://books.google.com/ngrams

More of historical value than practical keyword research value, this tool nonetheless allows you to input a keyword and see the historical rise or decline of a particular word. Sort of like Google Trends but longer term, and based on book content rather than web searches.

Rating: 2 Stars | **Category:** tool

YOAST KEYWORD SUGGEST TOOL - https://yoast.com/suggest/

Yet another tool based on Google suggest. The interface is not sexy and pizazzy (is that a word?), but it works.

Rating: 2 Stars | **Category:** tool

GOOGLE CORRELATE - http://google.com/trends/correlate

Built on Insights for Search, this tool attempts to allow you to enter a search term (say, 'Flowers') and find what other search terms correlate in search trend activity with that term. Not that useful (yet) but since trend spotting is a very important marketing tool, it does make our list.

Rating: 1 Stars | **Category:** tool

GOOGLE TRENDS - http://google.com/trends

Use Google's interface to monitor keyword trends! This free tool from Google allows you to enter keywords, select appropriate years and see search volume and related searches. Try 'cash for clunkers' or 'flowers' and look for trends across a given year. Sadly, this tool could be so, so very much more than the crippled functionality Google gives us.

Rating: 1 Stars | **Category:** tool

3

PAGE TAGS

HTML is the language of Google, and you must "speak HTML" to propel your pages to the top of Google, as well as the other search engines. It isn't enough to just write your pages in HTML; all web pages are in HTML, after all. Rather, you must **weave** your priority **keywords** into strategic page tags such as your <TITLE> tag, <H1>, or <A HREF> tags. Page tags communicate to Google what your page is "about" on a priority basis.

Here are the best **free** Page Tags tools on the Internet, ranked with the best tools first!

GOOGLE SEO STARTER GUIDE - http://bit.ly/google-seo-starter

This is the one, and only, really good resource by Google that is an official guide to what to do when, how, where and why for SEO. It covers mainly 'on page' SEO but definitely identifies basic tasks to accomplish on your website. Highly recommended.

Rating: 5 Stars | **Category:** resource

SEOCENTRO META TAG ANALYZER - http://seocentro.com/tools/search-engines/metatag-analyzer.html

SEOCentro designed this Meta Tag analysis tool to help webmasters analyze their web pages. This tool analyzes not only Meta Tags but where your keywords are positioned on the page, plus provides information on keyword density. When using Firefox, use CTRL+F to highlight your keywords in the results. In doing so, you can quickly check to see if a target keyword is well positioned vis-a-vis important tags like the TITLE or META DESCRIPTION tag.

Rating: 5 Stars | **Category:** tool

SIDE-BY-SIDE SEO COMPARISON TOOL - http://internetmarketingninjas.com/seo-tools/seo-compare

Wondering why two pages rank differently on Google search? Enter the URL of each page, and this nifty tool compares them using on page SEO. (Remember, of course, that off page (links) are incredibly important as well).

Rating: 4 Stars | **Category:** tool

TITLE TAG EVALUATION TOOL - http://nightbirdwebsolutions.com/title_creator_tool.php

This tool will evaluate how your existing Title tag relates to the content on the page, and it can suggest an order for the words based upon your content. The tool can also evaluate a new web page title to compare to an existing title.

Rating: 4 Stars | **Category:** tool

KEYWORD DENSITY CHECKER - KEYWORD CLOUD - http://webconfs.com/keyword-density-checker.php

This tool provides two perspectives on keyword density. Enter a URL and this tool will create a Keyword Cloud and provide a Keyword Density listing. A Keyword Cloud is a visual depiction of keywords used on a website. Keywords having higher density are depicted in a larger fonts. Ideally your main keywords should appear in larger fonts at the start of the cloud. The Keyword Density listing is a list of all keywords on the page ordered by count and density percentage. You can also pop a competitor in here to get keyword ideas!

Rating: 4 Stars | **Category:** tool

SEO TAG COUNTER TOOLS - http://nightbirdwebsolutions.com/tools/title-description-tag-free-counter-tool

The TITLE tag should be less than 69 visible characters. The META DESCRIPTION should be less than 155 characters. This free tool allows you to input your text and count it automatically. Great for using as you write these two important META TAGS for SEO.

Rating: 4 Stars | **Category:** tool

SEOCENTRO KEYWORD DENSITY TOOL - http://seocentro.com/tools/seo/keyword-density.html

One element critical to SEO success is having good keyword density. A page that has good keyword density - such as three to seven percent of content - will outrank a page with lower density, all things considered. However, you also don't want to go overboard and have too many keywords. Input a web URL into this tool and it generates a cool 'keyword cloud' as well as helping you see the density.

Rating: 4 Stars | **Category:** tool

ON-PAGE OPTIMIZATION TOOL - http://internetmarketingninjas.com/seo-tools/free-optimization

This web page optimization tool analyzes existing on-page SEO and lets you see your website as a spider sees it and allows for better web page optimization. This tool is helpful for analyzing your internal links, meta information and page content to develop better on-page SEO.

Rating: 3 Stars | **Category:** tool

SCHEMA CREATOR - http://schema-creator.org

Schemas are new microdata that allow you to 'communicate' with Google what a page is about. This nifty tool allows you to build your own schema on the fly, without having to understand all that pesky nerd data like what is microdata, anyway?

Rating: 3 Stars | **Category:** tool

WORD COUNTER - https://wordcounter.net/

Counts words and characters. Useful for SEO, especially TITLE and META DESCRIPTION tags for which limited characters are displayed in search results.

Rating: 3 Stars | **Category:** tool

TAGCROWD - http://tagcrowd.com

Input your website URL or any URL, and this nifty program will create a tag cloud of keywords density on your site. It's a useful self-check for keywords / keyword density.

Rating: 3 Stars | **Category:** tool

WORD COUNT - http://wordcountertool.com

This nifty tool will count your characters as you type. Remember that an optimal TITLE tag is less than 80 characters, with only the first 69 or so visible on Google. An optimal META DESCRIPTION tag is 155 characters.

Rating: 3 Stars | **Category:** tool

LETTER COUNTER - http://www.lettercount.com/

The TITLE tag should be LESS THAN 80 characters, with the MOST IMPORTANT being the first 66 characters. Your META DESCRIPTION should be less than 155 characters. Use this nifty online tool to copy / paste your tag text and it will automatically count it for you (characters and spaces).

Rating: 3 Stars | **Category:** tool

BRUCE CLAY'S SEOTOOLSET TOOLS - http://seotoolset.com/tools/free_tools.html

Bruce Clay is a guru in Search Engine Optimization. Use this page to access many of his free tools. The best are: Single Page Analyzer, Link Analysis Report, Keyword Suggestion Tool. Useful primarily for keyword discovery and checking your page tags vs. target keywords.

Rating: 2 Stars | **Category:** tool

PHPJABBERS SEO TOOL - http://phpjabbers.com/seo-tool.php

This is another SEO analysis tool. Enter your URL and then it analyzes the on-page SEO aspects of the page.

Rating: 2 Stars | **Category:** tool

SEO QUAKE - http://www.seoquake.com/

Many people love this SEO tool, a plugin for Firefox. Once you install it, you have a toolbar wherein you can search the web, look at competitors, and view their PageRank, link analysis, keywords, etc. It also alters how your Google appears. Decide if you like it. It can be overwhelming.

Rating: 2 Stars | **Category:** tool

GOOGLE SEO CHEAT SHEET -
http://googlewebmastercentral.blogspot.com/2013/03/cheat-sheet-for-friends-and-family.html

This Google Webmaster Here is Google's one page SEO cheat sheet. This is a VERY basic guide to SEO, especially on page. Note: it's a PDF file but sometimes it doesn't show up like that when you download it. So you may have to "tell" your PC / MAC that it's a PDF file.

Rating: 2 Stars | **Category:** book

FREE SEO SCORECARD - http://freeseoscorecard.com

This is a quick tool for on page SEO analysis. It's a bit campy and annoying but does provide the page entered a score, and some helpful hints on tag basics.

Rating: 2 Stars | **Category:** tool

PINEBERRY SEO ANALYSIS TOOL - http://pineberry.com/en/analysis-tool

This nifty little tool allows you to enter a page URL and a target keyword. It then will compare your target keyword vs. the on page aspects such as your tag structure, keyword density, etc. Good for a quick heads up analyzing your page content vs. target keywords.

Rating: 2 Stars | **Category:** tool

4

LINK BUILDING

Links are the votes of the Web. Google and the other search engines richly reward sites that enjoy many high quality links from high authority web pages. How do you identify link targets? How can you measure PageRank?

Here are the best **free** link-building tools on the Internet, ranked with the best tools first!

OPENLINKPROFILER - http://openlinkprofiler.org

> FREE tool for backlink analysis. Input your site, or that of a competitor, and see NEW links to that site. What's great is that it focuses on newly found links, not just all links, so that gives it a unique niche in the crowded field of backlink analysis tools. It also alerts to you to anchor texts and suspicious links.
>
> **Rating:** 5 Stars | **Category:** tool

BUZZSUMO - http://buzzsumo.com

> Buzzsumo is a 'buzz' monitoring tool for social media. Input a website (domain) and/or a topic and see what people are sharing across Facebook, Twitter, Google+ and other social media. Great for link-building (because what people link to is what they share), and also for social media.
>
> **Rating:** 5 Stars | **Category:** tool

MOZ: OPEN SITE EXPLORER - https://moz.com/researchtools/ose/

> This wonderful tool tells you who links to whom on the Internet. Enter a URL and the tool will then identify backlinks to that URL. Input your own website and check up how many links you have; enter a competitor, and 'reverse engineer' who links to them.
>
> **Rating:** 5 Stars | **Category:** tool

AHREFS - https://ahrefs.com/

> AHrefs takes its name from the A HREF element/attribute (i.e., HTML hyperlink tag). This tool helps you investigate links and link-building issues for any website. A useful tool to use in companion with Open Site Explorer. You can also use it to reverse engineer competitor keywords.
>
> **Rating:** 5 Stars | **Category:** tool

TOPSY - http://topsy.com

Real-time Twitter search engine. You can also search the web and videos. VERY important: you can input a URL, e.g., jm-seo.org or chipestimate.com, and see how frequently that URL and its sub URLs have been tweeted. Great way to see your social shares as well as discover what's trending on the blogosphere for more effective blogging.

Rating: 5 Stars | **Category:** engine

LINK BUILDING QUERY GENERATOR - http://tools.buzzstream.com/link-building-query-generator

Another input keywords and generate Google or Bing link tools. It creates an easy to use first step, but then you have to do the hard work to go and look for all those link targets!

Rating: 4 Stars | **Category:** tool

REMOVE'EM - https://www.removeem.com/ratios.php

This nifty tool analyzes your backlink profile and gives you some guidance if you have over-optimized your anchor text. Useful in the post-Penguin link environment.

Rating: 4 Stars | **Category:** tool

SOLO SEO LINK SEARCH TOOL - http://soloseo.com/tools/linkSearch.html

This simple, but nifty tool, will take a target keyword and generate a list of Google searches for blogs, catalogs, and other sorts of sites. Very simple, but very useful as a starting point on your link building exercise!

Rating: 4 Stars | **Category:** tool

SITEEXPLORER.INFO - http://siteexplorer.info

Yet another easy-to-use link building and exploration tool. Enter a URL and find who links to it.

Rating: 4 Stars | **Category:** tool

LINK BUILDING TACTICS - THE COMPLETE LIST - http://pointblankseo.com/link-building-strategies

This blog post isn't just about link building - it is link building. This massive list of ideas is massively linked to because, quite frankly, it's really good. Read this list and brainstorm your own link building tactics.

Rating: 4 Stars | **Category:** article

BACKLINK WATCH - http://backlinkwatch.com

Another checker of backlinks. Enter a website URL and this tool gives you a list of inbound links, after quite a few annoying ads. Still a useful tool.

Rating: 4 Stars | **Category:** tool

MAJESTIC SEARCH EXPLORER - http://majesticseo.com/reports/search-explorer

Who's winning at your keywords, and why? We know it's a function of a) on page SEO, and b) off page SEO, namely links. This incredible tool looks at the Google results for your keyword query, and shows the link score for the top players. A very revealing look at how links impact search engine results page ranking (SERP rank).

Rating: 4 Stars | **Category:** tool

LINK DIAGNOSIS - http://linkdiagnosis.com

This fantastic, free tool can show you all the important information about your competitor's links. The report includes PageRank, anchor text, no-follow information and more. You enter your website, wait (a long time) as it meticulously goes through link after link and ultimately provides a nice report about backlinks to your website (or better yet, that of your competitor). Can be downloaded for use in Firefox (only) or used on this website.

Rating: 4 Stars | **Category:** tool

MAJESTIC SEO - https://majestic.com/

This company provides some pretty good link checking tools. Nothing that you really can't get from other sites, in easier-to-use format. But still if you are really researching who links to whom - yourself vs. competitors, this tool is free and worth a look.

Rating: 4 Stars | **Category:** tool

BACKLINK EXPLORER - http://explorer.cognitiveseo.com/

This tool, based on a freemium model, allows a few 'free' back link searches - enough to see how you and your competitors align. Enter a URL, and see who links to whom.

Rating: 3 Stars | **Category:** tool

GUEST BLOG POST OPPORTUNITY FINDER - http://mangiamarketing.com/free-link-building-tools/guest-post-opportunity-finder

This nifty little tool takes your keywords and creates Google searches to help you find guest blogging opportunities.

Rating: 3 Stars | **Category:** tool

ALEXA - http://www.alexa.com/

Alexa is (yet another) search engine. One of its unique features is site statistics and traffic information for each returned item. You can use it, therefore, to 'reverse engineer' competitors. It also provides some inbound link data and keyword data for those competitors - so useful for link building research and competitive keyword research.

Rating: 3 Stars | **Category:** engine

CHARITY NAVIGATOR - http://www.charitynavigator.org/

Sponsoring charities, and getting links FROM the charity or non-profit to your website, is a great link-building technique. Use this site to find charities you might sponsor to receive links from in return.

Rating: 3 Stars | **Category:** resource

LIKE EXPLORER - http://www.likeexplorer.com/

Type in a URL and see its shares across social media outlets, including Facebook, Twitter, Google+, LinkedIn, Pinterest, and StumbleUpon. Very useful for link-building and competitor research.

Rating: 3 Stars | **Category:** tool

LINKARATI'S LINK BUILDING GUIDE (PAGEONEPOWER) - http://www.pageonepower.com/link-building-resources

OK, we've taken the (link)baitl. This article, once published by Literati and now owned by PagePower, is a compendium of both link-building tools AND points to deep-dive articles. Once you've graduated from the basics, dive in to topics such as link-bait, badge-bait, broken link building and more esoteric topics that separate the men from the boys, and women from the girls.

Rating: 3 Stars | **Category:** article

TALKWALKER ALERTS - http://www.talkwalker.com/alerts

Similar to Google Alerts, Talkwalker allows you to input your keywords, and then get alerts on new sites, and new mentions (e.g., a keyword or your brand name).

Rating: 3 Stars | **Category:** tool

TOUCH GRAPH LINK TOOL - http://touchgraph.com/seo

Based on Java, this visual tool allows you to input a domain or a keyword and see the top sites. It uses the 'related' syntax in Google search to find related websites to a keyword or domain. Technically the information retrieved isn't different than what you would get with the Google toolbar or the related syntax command...but a picture can say a thousand words. Visually stunning.

Rating: 3 Stars | **Category:** tool

FREE BACKLINK CHECKER - http://www.checkyourlinkpopularity.com/

This tool provides a quick look at the popularity of a website's inbound backlinks. It has some good information but some exceedingly ANNOYING advertising pop ups and gimmicks.

Rating: 2 Stars | **Category:** tool

PIKTOCHART - http://piktochart.com

Free infographic creator. Useful for blogging and creating 'link bait' for link building.

Rating: 2 Stars | **Category:** tool

SEO QUAKE - http://www.seoquake.com/

Many people love this SEO tool, a plugin for Firefox. Once you install it, you have a toolbar wherein you can search the web, look at competitors, and view their PageRank, link analysis, keywords, etc. It also alters how your Google appears. Decide if you like it. It can be overwhelming.

Rating: 2 Stars | **Category:** tool

SHARED COUNT - http://www.sharedcount.com/

This nifty tool will allow you to enter a URL (yours or that of a competitor) and then see the extent of social sharing across networks. It is useful both as a general sense of the social media buzz or social mentions around a domain, as well as for Link Building in a metric sense. (Who has more social mentions? Why?)

Rating: 2 Stars | **Category:** tool

MONITOR BACKLINKS - https://monitorbacklinks.com/seo-tools/free-backlink-checker

Yet another backlink checker; only provides a teeny-tiny taste of the backlinks, before you are required to register.

Rating: 2 Stars | **Category:** tool

SOCIAL MEDIA COUNT TOOL - https://varvy.com/tools/social/

Social mentions such as Google+ '+1s' or Facebook Likes are a newer form of links and link building. This tool allows you to enter a website, and see how shares it is has across social networks like Google+, Facebook, Twitter, LinkedIn, and Pinterest.

Rating: 2 Stars | **Category:** tool

5

CONTENT

Content is king – now more than ever. We have entered the era of "content marketing." For both SEO and SMM (Social Media Marketing) you need to create a content marketing system. Ranging from how you construct your home page, to how you build your anchor landing pages, to how you create a plethora of blog posts and other types of content – you gotta get content!

Here are the best **free** content marketing tools and services on the Internet, ranked with the best tools first!

TOPSY - http://topsy.com

Real-time Twitter search engine. You can also search the web and videos. VERY important: you can input a URL, e.g., jm-seo.org or chipestimate.com, and see how frequently that URL and its sub URLs have been tweeted. Great way to see your social shares as well as discover what's trending on the blogosphere for more effective blogging.

Rating: 5 Stars | **Category:** engine

FEEDLY - http://feedly.com

Feedly is a newsreader integrated with Google+ or Facebook. It's useful for social media because you can follow important blogs or other content and share it with your followers. It can also spur great blog ideas.

Rating: 5 Stars | **Category:** resource

BUZZSUMO - http://buzzsumo.com

Buzzsumo is a 'buzz' monitoring tool for social media. Input a website (domain) and/or a topic and see what people are sharing across Facebook, Twitter, Google+ and other social media. Great for link-building (because what people link to is what they share), and also for social media.

Rating: 5 Stars | **Category:** tool

YOUTUBE TOOLS - http://youtube.com/yt/creators/tools.html

YouTube has done more and more to make it easier to publish and promote videos. This page lists six tools: YouTube Capture, YouTube Editor, Captions, Audio Library, Slideshow and YouTube Analytics. All of them are fantastic, free tools about YouTube by YouTube.

Rating: 5 Stars | **Category:** resource

YOUTUBE CREATOR HUB - http://youtube.com/yt/creators

Help center for those creating YouTube content. Learn how to better edit your videos, get them up on YouTube, etc. Has lessons on growing your audience, boot camp, and how to get viewers and even how to earn money via YouTube.

Rating: 5 Stars | **Category:** resource

COMPFIGHT - http://compfight.com

Unclear where the name comes from, but no matter. This incredible tool allows you to search for royalty-based and royalty-free images. Great for finding images for blogging and posting to social media. Quickly locate royalty-free images!

Rating: 4 Stars | **Category:** service

FOTER - http://foter.com

Add some color (or monochrome) to your blog posts with Foter. Search over 200 million high-quality, free, downloadable stock photos. Don't forget to copy and paste photo attribution credits included with the images details into your blog post.

Rating: 4 Stars | **Category:** resource

GOOGLE EMAIL ALERTS - http://google.com/alerts

Use Google to alert you by email for search results that matter to you. Input your company name, for example, to see when new web pages, blog posts, or other items surface on the web. Enter your target keywords to keep an eye on yourself and your competitors. Part of the Gmail system.

Rating: 4 Stars | **Category:** service

PHOTOPIN - http://photopin.com

Get in the habit of creating blog posts with images by using PhotoPin. PhotoPin searches millions of Creative Commons photos and allows you to preview, download any of multiple sizes to upload into your posts, and provides handy cut and paste HTML for attribution, a small price to pay for royalty-free images. Adding images to your blog posts doesn't get any easier than this.

Rating: 4 Stars | **Category:** service

CREATIVE COMMONS SEARCH - http://search.creativecommons.org

Another resource to find royalty-free images, clip art, sound and music to share or utilize with other content. Great way to find shareable images to embed into blog posts.

Rating: 4 Stars | **Category:** resource

PIXLR - https://pixlr.com

Pixlr is a free, online photo editor. Great for social media post, to add that extra umph to any image more easily than in Adobe Photoshop.

Rating: 4 Stars | **Category:** tool

PABLO - https://buffer.com/pablo

Take an image, add some text. Presto! You have an engaging image for your blog post or social sharing. Memes, anyone?

Rating: 4 Stars | **Category:** tool

YOUTUBE CAPTURE - https://youtube.com/capture

YouTube Capture is an app for your mobile phone, which makes it easy to capture and edit videos right on your phone. Imagine you are a marketer / retailer and you want to use your phone to easily capture customer interactions, and upload (quickly / easily) to YouTube. Get the picture?

Rating: 4 Stars | **Category:** tool

QZZR - https://qzzr.com

Create online quizzes and share with your social network. What cat breed are you? If you were a Twilight character, which character would you be? Fun quizzes to encourage social sharing.

Rating: 4 Stars | **Category:** tool

YouTube Editor - https://youtube.com/editor

While there is Microsoft Windows Movie Maker and Apple iMovie, there is also a free YouTube editor for your videos. Not incredibly powerful, but free and easy to use 'in the cloud.'

Rating: 3 Stars | **Category:** tool

Easely - http://easel.ly

Use thousands of templates and design objects to easily create infographics for your blog.

Rating: 3 Stars | **Category:** tool

Pikiz - http://getpikiz.com

Take an image, add some text plus a lot of emotion and it might just go viral. This is a free / freemium image maker plus textifier. Memes, anyone?

Rating: 3 Stars | **Category:** tool

SlideShare - http://slideshare.net

PowerPoint slides for the Web. Create a "deck," upload it to SlideShare and have a) a place to put content in slide format, and b) a platform that can also lead to discoverability. PowerPoint on the Web, PowerPoint gone social.

Rating: 3 Stars | **Category:** tool

Meme Generator - http://memegenerator.net

Memes are shareable photos, usually with text. But how do you create them? Why, use memegenerator.net.

Rating: 3 Stars | **Category:** tool

CONTENT MARKETING WORLD - http://www.contentmarketingworld.com/

Content Marketing World is the one event where you can learn and network with the best and the brightest in the content marketing industry.You will leave with all the materials you need to take a content marketing strategy back to your team – and – to implement a content marketing plan that will grow your business and inspire your audience.

Rating: 3 Stars | **Category:** conference

PIXABAY - http://pixabay.com

Pixabay is a photo sharing community and a great source of royalty-free, attribution-free, stock images for your blog. Ignore the first row of sponsored images in the search results.

Rating: 3 Stars | **Category:** service

YOUZIGN - https://youzign.com

This is a 'Photoshop in the cloud' sort of tool. Use it to create visual art such as YouTube background art, infographics, Facebook cover photos, and other visual content for social media.

Rating: 3 Stars | **Category:** tool

WINDOWS MOVIE MAKER - http://windows.microsoft.com/en-us/windows-live/movie-maker

For those on the Windows platform, Movie Maker is the goto free program to edit videos for YouTube and other platforms.

Rating: 3 Stars | **Category:** tool

POWTOON - https://powtoon.com

PowToon provides animated video production using the freemium pricing model. Play around with it to create animated videos to present anything you want about your business. Paid plans available, but you can do some cool stuff for free.

Rating: 2 Stars | **Category:** tool

PIKTOCHART - http://piktochart.com

Free infographic creator. Useful for blogging and creating 'link bait' for link building.

Rating: 2 Stars | **Category:** tool

INFO.GRAM - https://infogr.am

Another free way to create infographics and charts. Free plan is limited to 10 infographics, 10 uploaded images, no private sharing and no downloads or live connections.

Rating: 2 Stars | **Category:** tool

PAPER.LI - http://paper.li

Create a curated set of content just for your audience. Paper.li is a content platform - you define what you want on a page, and it builds a custom newspaper on the Web for you (and your customers).

Rating: 2 Stars | **Category:** tool

BLOGS

With the advent of "real-time search," Google strongly rewards sites that blog. But beyond just having a blog and using "on page" SEO tactics, you can adjust your blog to make it a stronger link attractor. In addition, you can identify bloggers on the Web who might let you "guest blog" or serve as partner sites for your content. Blogging, like press releases, can be a bridge between your "on page" and "off page" SEO strategy.

Here are the best **free** SEO-friendly blog tools and services on the Internet, ranked with the best tools first!

SIMPLE GUIDE TO BUSINESS BLOGGING -
http://simplybusiness.co.uk/microsites/guide-business-blogging

> Interactive step-by-step guide to business blogging. Comprised of key questions and linked resources from around the web with more information. Thoughtful and well constructed.
>
> **Rating:** 4 Stars | **Category:** resource

COMPFIGHT - http://compfight.com

> Unclear where the name comes from, but no matter. This incredible tool allows you to search for royalty-based and royalty-free images. Great for finding images for blogging and posting to social media. Quickly locate royalty-free images!
>
> **Rating:** 4 Stars | **Category:** service

BLOG POST HEADLINE ANALYZER - http://coschedule.com/headline-analyzer

> Want to write better blog headlines? Use the Blog Post Headline Analyzer to get a feel for how effective your blog post headlines are. This tool analyzes entered headlines across numerous criteria including keywords, sentiment, structure, grammar, and readability to produce a headline score in an attractive graphical format. Try it and see.
>
> **Rating:** 4 Stars | **Category:** tool

FOTER - http://foter.com

> Add some color (or monochrome) to your blog posts with Foter. Search over 200 million high-quality, free, downloadable stock photos. Don't forget to copy and paste photo attribution credits included with the images details into your blog post.
>
> **Rating:** 4 Stars | **Category:** resource

BLOG TOPIC GENERATOR - http://hubspot.com/blog-topic-generator

If you're hurting for blog topic ideas, try this fun tool from HubSpot. Enter three nouns, then watch the tool generate a weeks worth of blog topics. If none of the generated topics pique your interest, hit the back key and try, try again until one does.

Rating: 4 Stars | **Category:** tool

ICEROCKET - http://icerocket.com

IceRocket is a very good blog search engine. Don't miss the Trend Tool that allows you to enter a keyword and watch trends.

Rating: 4 Stars | **Category:** engine

PHOTOPIN - http://photopin.com

Get in the habit of creating blog posts with images by using PhotoPin. PhotoPin searches millions of Creative Commons photos and allows you to preview, download any of multiple sizes to upload into your posts, and provides handy cut and paste HTML for attribution, a small price to pay for royalty-free images. Adding images to your blog posts doesn't get any easier than this.

Rating: 4 Stars | **Category:** service

CREATIVE COMMONS SEARCH - http://search.creativecommons.org

Another resource to find royalty-free images, clip art, sound and music to share or utilize with other content. Great way to find shareable images to embed into blog posts.

Rating: 4 Stars | **Category:** resource

LINKEDIN PULSE - https://www.linkedin.com/today/posts

Need ideas for your next blog post? Look no further than LinkedIn Pulse where top business influencers post their thoughts daily. Handy drop-down selector at right allows you to see Top Posts from today, this week, and all time. Click the Discover Tab to customize your Pulse feed with influencers relevant to your interests.

Rating: 4 Stars | **Category:** resource

TWEAK YOUR BIZ TITLE GENERATOR - http://tweakyourbiz.com/tools/title-generator/index.php

Good blog post TITLES are critical. You should include your keywords for SEO purposes, but add some pizazz, some sex appeal, some please-click-me oomph. This nifty tool gets your ideas flowing for good TITLES.

Rating: 4 Stars | **Category:** tool

WORDPRESS PLUGIN DIRECTORY - http://wordpress.org/plugins

WordPress is the most popular blogging platform. This is their complete directory of plugins. Don't forget to install an SEO plugin to improve your searchability!

Rating: 4 Stars | **Category:** resource

PIXLR - https://pixlr.com

Pixlr is a free, online photo editor. Great for social media post, to add that extra umph to any image more easily than in Adobe Photoshop.

Rating: 4 Stars | **Category:** tool

BLOG SEARCH ENGINE - http://www.blogsearchengine.org/

Now that Google has discontinued its own blog search engine,how does one identify possible bloggers? Enter Blog Search Engine, one of the best ways to identify blog posts and blogs vs. your target keywords.

Rating: 4 Stars | **Category:** engine

YOAST - http://yoast.com

Yoast is the No. 1 recommended SEO plugin for WordPress. Highly recommended, as it adds needed functionality to WordPress such as splitting the

TITLE tag from the Post TITLE, META description, and a nice 'focus' tool to analyze how well your post is optimized for on page SEO vs. a target keyword.

Rating: 4 Stars | **Category:** tool

FACEBOOK COMMENTS PLUGIN -
https://developers.facebook.com/docs/plugins/comments

Want more comments on your blog? Want people who comment to have those comments go viral? This Facebook Plugin makes it easy for people to comment on your blog, no more annoying double registration, plus if they comment you can encourage them to post the comment to their Facebook page - hence, viral marketing!

Rating: 4 Stars | **Category:** tool

PORTENT CONTENT IDEA GENERATOR - http://portent.com/tools/title-maker

Very fun and mind-provocative tool for content ideas and better blog titles. Enter some keywords and the tool will generate some funny titles. So start with keywords and then generate your amazingly, funny and hypnotic blog titles. These then become the HEADLINES on Google by which you can attract more clicks!

Rating: 4 Stars | **Category:** tool

GUEST BLOG POST OPPORTUNITY FINDER - http://mangiamarketing.com/free-link-building-tools/guest-post-opportunity-finder

This nifty little tool takes your keywords and creates Google searches to help you find guest blogging opportunities.

Rating: 3 Stars | **Category:** tool

COPYSCAPE - http://copyscape.com

Since Google can penalize websites with plagiarized content, avoid being penalized for someone stealing your content with Copyscape. Enter the page URL and Copyscape will return pages which may have duplicated its content.

Copyscape even provides some tips and resources should content have been plagiarized.

Rating: 3 Stars | **Category:** tool

PITCHERIFIC - https://pitcherific.com

Blogging is a lot like 'pitching' clients. You need a good headline, an angle on why this is important, often you are 'solving' a 'problem' with a 'solution.' This fun tool will help you devise a pitch, which could also become a great blog post.

Rating: 3 Stars | **Category:** tool

ULTIMATE HEADLINE FORMULAS - https://blog.bufferapp.com/headline-formulas

If you've wondered how to create headlines for blog posts, articles, emails, etc., which will entice readers to click and read on, this article gathers a gaggle of formulas from some of the best sources for headline writing in one place. It also includes a free, downloadable PDF of the best headline formulas.

Rating: 3 Stars | **Category:** article

WORDPRESS SEO TUTORIAL - http://yoast.com/articles/wordpress-seo

This is a very good guide for WordPress SEO using the Yoast plugin. It covers only the technical issues, however, but when combined with our classes and an understanding of keyword research, website structure, and off-page SEO link building - this guide is very helpful for crossing the t's and dotting the i's of a strong SEO-friendly WordPress website.

Rating: 3 Stars | **Category:** resource

PIXABAY - http://pixabay.com

Pixabay is a photo sharing community and a great source of royalty-free, attribution-free, stock images for your blog. Ignore the first row of sponsored images in the search results.

Rating: 3 Stars | **Category:** service

BLOGGER - http://blogger.com

Need a blog? Google's Blogger platform, sometimes referred to as Blogspot, while not as pervasive as WordPress, is quick, easy, and very SEO friendly. If you want a straightforward, hosted, business blog, Blogger might be a better choice than WordPress.com. You can even attach a domain!

Rating: 3 Stars | **Category:** service

WORDPRESS SUPPORT - http://wordpress.org/support

WordPress is the No. 1 blogging platform but it is anything but simple or intuitive. Use the support site to 'get started' with WordPress as a blogging platform, as well as to learn the more esoteric elements of WordPress.

Rating: 3 Stars | **Category:** resource

TWITTERFEED - http://twitterfeed.com

Feed your blog to Twitter, Facebook, LinkedIn and other social networks, automagically.

Rating: 2 Stars | **Category:** service

HEADLINE GENERATOR - http://internetmarketingcourse.com/freeheadlinegenerator

Got writer's block? Wondering how to generate a snazzy headline for a product page, blog post, or even news release? Answer a few questions about your blog post or product page, and this tool will generate a list of suggested headlines.

Rating: 2 Stars | **Category:** tool

7

PRESS RELEASES

Press Releases are an underutilized form of SEO. With the advent of "real-time search" and syndication services like PRWEB.com, Google rewards sites that have frequent press releases and blog posts. First, it rewards them with links from the Google search page directly to their press releases and blog posts - especially if they are created in an SEO-friendly way. Second, press releases can be part of your "link-building" strategy. And third, Google rewards sites with frequent, keyword-heavy press releases *that are Panda- and Penguin-compatible*, with a "better reputation" and thereby more frequent spidering. It's a three-for-one benefit!

Here are the best **free** press release syndication tools on the Internet, ranked with the best services first!

PRWeb - http://www.prweb.com/

Not free, but inexpensive, PRWeb does an excellent job of taking your news release and syndicating it across the Internet. For about $200, you can reach thousands of websites, blogs, portals and other media plus encourage Google to index your news release and new content. Because it is so good, we make an exception to our general rule of only identifying free resources. Well worth $200.

Rating: 5 Stars | **Category:** service

PRLog Press Release Distribution - http://www.prlog.org/

PRLog is a free online press release service. First, create your press release on your own website in SEO-friendly HTML. Second, log in to your free PRLog.org account. Third, input your press release for distribution. Fourth, publish! This free service is a fantastic way to syndicate your press release, gain instant links, encourage Google to index your website and more. News is still an effective way to boost SEO!

Rating: 5 Stars | **Category:** service

PressReleasePoint - http://www.pressreleasepoint.com/

PressReleasePoint offers both free and paid distribution services. PressReleasePoint.com is a free press release distribution website to connect PR professionals with journalists and media outlets. Online marketers can generate media visibility and maximize online presence by distributing press release through PressReleasePoint.

Rating: 5 Stars | **Category:** service

Help a Reporter Out (HARO) - http://www.helpareporter.com/

A service journalists use to put queries out into the ether. Sign up to receive queries from working journalists, and then 'pitch' them on contacting you and your company, usually as an expert.

Rating: 4 Stars | **Category:** service

INSTANT PRESS RELEASE TOOL - http://ducttapemarketing.com/IPR.htm

This tool from Duct Tape Marketing helps you write a draft press release. Enter the city, state, headline, first paragraphs, etc. and presto, see your press release instantly!

Rating: 4 Stars | **Category:** tool

ONLINE PR MEDIA - http://www.onlineprnews.com/

Online PR Media, in its own humble words, is the premier source for publishing SEO press releases. After years of research (again in their own humble words) we've combined all of the features that Internet marketers, business owners, and journalists have asked for in an online press release distribution site. Has a limited free service.

Rating: 4 Stars | **Category:** service

PRESS ABOUT - http://www.pressabout.com/

Press About is a paid, but very inexpensive, press release service. The cost is just about $9.00. The site does appear to allow 'followed' links in press releases via a JavaScript link tracking mechanism.

Rating: 3 Stars | **Category:** service

EMAILWIRE - http://emailwire.com

EmailWire is a press release distribution service. The basic fee is $99.00.

Rating: 3 Stars | **Category:** service

PRESSEXPOSURE - http://pressexposure.com/

PressExposure.com is the place where companies, organizations and individuals can submit their press releases for distribution FREE.

Rating: 3 Stars | **Category:** service

24-7 PRESS RELEASES - http://www.24-7pressrelease.com/

Yet another press release distribution service. Most plans are paid, but does offer a limited free trial plan which includes one free press release per day.

Rating: 3 Stars | **Category:** service

PR URGENT NEWS - http://prurgent.com

Free press release and news distribution website which publishes high quality press releases, which will get you visibility in major search engines and news sites including Google News, MSN, Yahoo, Bing and others.

Rating: 2 Stars | **Category:** service

BRIEFINGWIRE - http://briefingwire.com

Free press release distribution service. Basic and to-the-point.

Rating: 2 Stars | **Category:** service

ERELEASES - http://www.ereleases.com/

A relatively expensive news release distribution service, eReleases has a strong affiliation with the AP wire service and PR Newswire. Competes with PRWeb.

Rating: 2 Stars | **Category:** service

RELEASE NEWS - http://www.release-news.com/

Release News is an online news submission and press release distribution service. It submits news releases to Google News and up to 1500+ major news syndications (including TV, newspapers, and radio), depending on plan purchased. Free plan only includes release on their website.

Rating: 2 Stars | **Category:** service

CLICKPRESS - http://www.clickpress.com/

ClickPress offers free press release distribution. Once news submitted to ClickPress has been approved, it is available not only to site visitors, but also to major web and news search engines. All submissions are free and news releases remain in searchable archives indefinitely.

Rating: 1 Stars | **Category:** service

THE OPEN PRESS - http://www.theopenpress.com/

The Open Press claims not to be just another free press release portal. They claim to have done their homework and market research and have spoken with journalists and industry professionals to get their feedback. They have standards for press releases and don't allow unprofessional press releases to be submitted. All free press releases must comply with press release guidelines.

Rating: 1 Stars | **Category:** service

NewswireTODAY - http://www.newswiretoday.com/

Press release distribution service. Service is FREE of charge for basic inclusion. PREMIUM inclusion offers logo placement, product image, highlighted text on home, real-time statistics tracker.

Rating: 1 Stars | **Category:** service

8

RANK

SEO is a lot like physical fitness! Just as you should measure your "Body Mass Index" (BMI), **before, during**, and **after** your fitness program, so you should measure your "Rank" on Google **before, during**, and **after** your SEO fitness efforts. The fact that your rank can vary greatly depending on your target keywords complicates rank measurement, but fortunately there are some great tools for automating this process. You can incorporate your rank measurement to identify strengths and weakness in your SEO strategy. Finally, if you are conducting paid AdWords advertising, you can feed your rank data into AdWords and thereby build on your SEO strengths and "target" your weaknesses for advertising support.

Here are the best **free** rank-checking tools on the Internet, ranked with the best tools first!

SEOBook Firefox Rank Checker Extension - http://tools.seobook.com/firefox/rank-checker/

Sign up for a free account, and you can use this tool to track your rank on Google and other search engines. It works only on Firefox, so be sure to install Firefox first. Then, here are the steps. First, input your domain - be sure to use lower case. Second, input your keyword list. Third, input any competitor names. This handy tool will track your SERP rank (your position on a Google search). You need to be in the top ten.

Rating: 5 Stars | **Category:** tool

Sitemapdoc SERP Rank Checker - http://sitemapdoc.com/Serp-Rank.aspx

This easy-to-use rank checking tool makes our list of the best easy SEO tools out there. Simply input your URL and a target keyword, and the tool quickly tells you your rank out of the top 64 sites. Easy, useful, free, and fun!

Rating: 5 Stars | **Category:** tool

Local Rank Checking via AdWords - https://adwords.google.com/apt/AdPreview

This is the OFFICIAL Google AdWords preview tool. But, guess what. You can use this to vary your city location, and check your rank against various cities. If, for example, you are a pizza restaurant serving San Jose, Milpitas, and Santa Clara, you can type in 'Pizza' and see your rank in different cities. You can login to your AdWord account and click Tools - Preview Tool or use this direct link.

Rating: 4 Stars | **Category:** tool

SEM Rush - http://www.semrush.com/

Similar to KeywordSpy, this tool allows you to enter a domain or a competitor, and returns a list of AdWords keywords they are running under as well as their organic keywords. Use it to track a competitor, as well as to generate a keyword list (keyword discovery).

Rating: 4 Stars | **Category:** tool

CUTERANK - http://cuterank.net

> CuteRank is a download-only tool that will allow you to input ONE domain for free and then measure its rank, over time. It's a pretty good tool, though not as useful as SEOCentro PageRank Checker.
>
> **Rating:** 4 Stars | **Category:** tool

SERPLAB RANK CHECKER - https://www.serplab.co.uk/serp-check.php

> Enter your domain AND some keywords, and this tool will tell you your rank. A bit slow to use, but pretty accurate.
>
> **Rating:** 3 Stars | **Category:** tool

SEOCENTRO RANK CHECKER - http://seocentro.com/tools/search-engines/keyword-position.html

> This online tool allows you to input your domain as well as that of a competitor and a keyword. It then quickly tells you your rank (SERP) on Google, Yahoo, and Bing. Not as robust as the Firefox Rank Checker extension from SEOBook, but a very quick and easy way to check your SERPs.
>
> **Rating:** 3 Stars | **Category:** tool

DYNAMIC KEYWORD GENERATOR TOOL - http://rustybrick.com/keyword-phrase-tool.php

> This tool enables you to enter your primary, secondary and even tertiary keyword phrases separated by comma (,) into the appropriate fields and click Generate Keywords to receive a robust list of keywords to copy and paste into your program of choice. For rank-checking, it makes it easy to generate a longer keyword list.
>
> **Rating:** 3 Stars | **Category:** tool

BING IT ON - BING VS. GOOGLE - http://bingiton.com

This site, created by Microsoft, allows you to compare Google and Bing search results. Input search terms and see Bing results vs. Google results side-by-side, leaving you to guess which is which. Snazzy, quick way to compare the two major search engine providers side by side.

Rating: 3 Stars | **Category:** tool

DELETE DUPLICATES KEYWORD TOOL - http://angular.marketing/free-tools/delete-duplicates

If you are building a long list for rank-checking, or for AdWords input, you often will unknowingly generate duplicates. Then when you pull your reports, they will often not correspond to your original, because rank checker and other tools auto-delete duplicates. Use this tool to prevent this from happening in the first place.

Rating: 3 Stars | **Category:** tool

HIDE MY ASS - https://www.hidemyass.com/

Despite the crude name, this is actually a useful service. It allows you to work around Google's pesky personalization by surfing privately. Enter your search terms and see what Google returns WITHOUT personalization / your physical location, etc.

Rating: 2 Stars | **Category:** service

KEYWORD POSITION TOOL - http://smallseotools.com/keyword-position

Another quick and dirty keyword rank checker. Enter your keywords and your domain...and this free tool will check your position in the top search engines for specific keywords to determine what is working, and what needs more work on your website.

Rating: 2 Stars | **Category:** tool

9

DIAGNOSTICS

"To diagnose" means to identify the nature of an illness or other problem by the nature of the symptoms. For your website as a whole and for your SEO efforts, effective diagnostic tools can not only identify when you have a problem but tell you what that problem is and even guide you to possible solutions.

Here are the best **free** diagnostic tools on the Internet, ranked with the best tools first!

WooRank - https://www.woorank.com/

Assuming you know some SEO (especially page tags), this really slick tool will take a web URL (such as your home page) and generate a quick report. HubSpot has a similar tool, but this tool is way cooler and faster! Then, use the report to check your website. Are you using the proper tags? Do the keywords you need show up in the correct spaces? A powerful free tool in the hands of someone who is SEO educated.

Rating: 5 Stars | **Category:** tool

Google Search Console (Webmaster Tools) - https://www.google.com/webmasters/

Google Webmaster Tools provides detailed reports about your pages' visibility on Google. To get started, simply add and verify your site and begin seeing information right away. Get Google's view of your site and diagnose problems. See how Google crawls and indexes your site and learn about specific problems they're having accessing it. Discover your link and query traffic. Also contains an extensive education section with videos and articles to help you get found on Google.

Rating: 5 Stars | **Category:** tool

Google PageSpeed Insights - https://developers.google.com/speed/pagespeed/insights

Use this Google tool to measure how fast your website is. Size might not matter, but speed does. Google likes speedy websites! It gives you a score, plus recommendations on what you can do to speed up your website. Not just what's wrong, but what to fix. Cool tool.

Rating: 4 Stars | **Category:** tool

Found SEO Tool - http://found.co.uk/seo-tool

This all-in-one SEO website checkup tool gives you not only on page information, but checks things such as canonical domain issues. It also access Moz's link database and provides some basic inbound link analysis for free.

Rating: 4 Stars | **Category:** tool

FEEDTHEBOT ANALYSIS TOOL - https://varvy.com/

How well does your website follow the Google Webmaster Guidelines? This all-in-one SEO analysis of your website will tell you. This site also has quite a few other microtools that are pretty good.

Rating: 4 Stars | **Category:** tool

IS IT HACKED? - http://isithacked.com/

Has your website been hacked? The funny thing is it may have been hacked, and yet you won't know. Hackers often inject hidden code and links into your site. If Google finds these, it may harshly penalize your rank on searches. So it's a good idea to check.

Rating: 4 Stars | **Category:** tool

PINGDOM TOOLS - http://tools.pingdom.com/

Diagnostic tools, such as how fast your website loads, and the DNS health of your domain name. Useful for optimizing your website performance which is increasingly important to Google. Speed, baby, speed (matters).

Rating: 4 Stars | **Category:** tool

COMPLEX SEO AUDIT - http://www.seomastering.com/

Want to know where your website is really hosted in the physical world? How fast it is? What the keywords it appears to be targeting. This nifty tool answers all those questions.

Rating: 4 Stars | **Category:** tool

GOOGLE SITE: SEARCH OPERATOR - http://google.com/search?q=site%3Ajm-seo.org

Use the site: search operator on Google to find out a) how many pages of your website are in the Google index (the first step towards getting to the top of Google), and b) to see your indexing patterns. Simply click on the left column, 'Show Search Tools,' and browse by week, month, day to see how frequently Google is indexing your website. You can 'train' Google to index your site more frequently!

Rating: 3 Stars | **Category:** tool

SEARCH ENGINE WATCH SEO TOOL - http://seotool.searchenginewatch.com

This tool requires registration and then does a nice analysis of your own site as well as competitors. One nice feature is that it asks you to identify target keywords and phrases, and then analyzes your performance based on that input. Requires a login, but a good free tool.

Rating: 3 Stars | **Category:** tool

SERPSTAT - http://serpstat.com/

Enter your domain (or that of a competitor) and see an analysis of your SEO competitive position. Useful to find out who competes with whom, and then to use that competitive set for keywords and link research.

Rating: 3 Stars | **Category:** tool

SIMILARWEB - http://similarweb.com

Unlike other monitoring tools previously mentioned, SimilarWeb monitors your competition's website. Use this tool to find out how your competitors are doing, see how much traffic they get and where it comes from. A great tool for anyone with some competition, aka everyone.

Rating: 3 Stars | **Category:** tool

CHECK SITE INFO - http://www.freewebsitetool.net/

Check your site, or a competitor's, for technical information. Will tell you the IP address, where it's hosted, and some basic technical information about the website.

Rating: 3 Stars | **Category:** tool

IP ADDRESS BLACKLIST CHECKER TOOL - http://www.ipvoid.com/

If your website traffic goes way, way down, it can indicate your site may have been infected with malware. This tool will check if your IP address has been listed on various Internet blacklists.

Rating: 3 Stars | **Category:** tool

SEOPTIMER - http://www.seoptimer.com/

Another all-in-one diagnostic tool. Enter a website address, click Analyze, and it will give you feedback, including some interesting data on 'social shares' such as Facebook, Twitter, and Google+.

Rating: 3 Stars | **Category:** tool

GEOPEEKER - https://geopeeker.com

Measure how fast your website loads in various places in the world. Great as a testing tool for website loading speed and performance.

Rating: 3 Stars | **Category:** service

GTMETRIX - https://gtmetrix.com/

Slow website got you down? Want to go mobile? Already gone mobile, but your site is terribly slow? This diagnostics tool helps you understand what's wrong (and then fix it). Submit your site, and then give the report to your developer to fix.

Rating: 3 Stars | **Category:** resource

SUCURI MALWARE CHECK - https://sitecheck.sucuri.net/

If your website is infected with malware, Google will quickly block you - creating a catastrophic drop in your rank on Google. This tool pre-scans your website for malware and infections, so you can see minute-by-minute if you have an issue.

Rating: 3 Stars | **Category:** tool

MOBILE-FRIENDLY TEST - https://www.google.com/webmasters/tools/mobile-friendly/

The mobile web is now so pervasive, many designers take a mobile-first design approach. Evaluate your existing web pages for mobile-friendliness with Google's Mobile-Friendly Tool. It analyzes a URL and reports if the page has a mobile-friendly design, per Google standards. You'll be glad you did.

Rating: 3 Stars | **Category:** tool

BUILTWITH - http://builtwith.com/

Useful for competitive analysis, this free tool takes a competitor website and analyzes the technologies it was 'built with.' It also highlights advertising technologies used (e.g., Google remarketing) and the hosting system they employ.

Rating: 2 Stars | **Category:** tool

HUBSPOT MARKETING GRADER - https://marketing.grader.com/

HubSpot sells HubSpot software, which isn't the best in my book. It's a bit of reselling stuff you can do on your own, and fluffing it up to make it look more important than it is. That said, they do have a nice all-in-one analysis tool. It tends to focus on on page, just a little bit on links, and way way too much on Twitter. But still it's fun and informative.

Rating: 2 Stars | **Category:** tool

GODADDY WHOIS - https://who.godaddy.com/

WhoIs provides basic information about who registered a domain. Also useful to identify available domain names as you brainstorm new ones.

Rating: 2 Stars | **Category:** tool

WEBPAGETEST - http://www.webpagetest.org/

If you are having page speed issues, this tool will take your website and analyze how fast it loads by constituent part. You can then reverse-engineer what parts load slowly vs. quickly, and optimize accordingly.

Rating: 2 Stars | **Category:** tool

ZADROWEB SEO AUDITOR - https://zadroweb.com/seo-auditor/

This quick and easy SEO audit tool provides only basic data. Unfortunately, it does not allow you to enter a keyword or group of keywords and compare / contrast your web page to that target.

Rating: 1 Stars | **Category:** tool

JUXSEO SEO REPORT - https://juxseo.zoomshift.com/

Another all-in-one review site for on page SEO. Enter your keyword and URL and the tool analyzes how well you have performed on page SEO.

Rating: 1 Stars | **Category:** tool

WEBSITE STRUCTURE

Website structure - the "organization" of your website - is an advanced element in effective SEO. While good page tags and link-building are more important and more powerful, effective website structure can mean the difference between securing Page 1 Position 1 and being downgraded to Page 3 Position 4, especially for "highly competitive" keywords. How you name your files, how you "reach out" to Google, and how you optimize your landing pages all combine to make a good SEO strategy, great!

Here are the best **free** website structure tools on the Internet, ranked with the best tools first!

GOOGLE SEARCH CONSOLE (WEBMASTER TOOLS) -
https://www.google.com/webmasters/

Google Webmaster Tools provides detailed reports about your pages' visibility on Google. To get started, simply add and verify your site and begin seeing information right away. Get Google's view of your site and diagnose problems. See how Google crawls and indexes your site and learn about specific problems they're having accessing it. Discover your link and query traffic. Also contains an extensive education section with videos and articles to help you get found on Google.

Rating: 5 Stars | **Category:** tool

BING WEBMASTER TOOLS - http://bing.com/toolbox/webmaster

Interested in Bing? This is the Bing Webmaster Tools home page. Similar to the Google suite. Has some new features that are radically improving this tool from Bing. Includes a good keyword discovery tool.

Rating: 5 Stars | **Category:** tool

XML SITEMAPS GENERATOR - https://www.xml-sitemaps.com/

Create sitemaps for Google, MSN and Yahoo! - the easy way! If you own or maintain a website or intend to own one, wouldn't it be great if you get frequent visitors who find satisfaction in getting exactly the information they need from your page? This free tool will index a site up to 500 pages and create your XMl site map for you. Then simply upload to your site, and tell Google it exists via Webmaster tools. Presto!

Rating: 5 Stars | **Category:** tool

GOOGLE WEBMASTER ACADEMY -
http://support.google.com/webmasters/answer/6001102

Google's learning site for SEO. Basic stuff, and a bit salesy, but a good starting point. Just remember who's talking - Google - and take it all with a grain of salt.

Rating: 5 Stars | **Category:** resource

GOOGLE WEBMASTERS YOUTUBE CHANNEL - http://youtube.com/googlewebmasterhelp

If you are a webmaster or someone interested in search engine optimization, this is a great site of YouTube videos created by Google. Of course it is the 'party line' from the biggest player in search - dare we say, the view of the search monopolist on what constitutes acceptable behavior? Especially useful on technical website structure issues.

Rating: 4 Stars | **Category:** video

FREE SITEMAP GENERATOR - https://freesitemapgenerator.com/

This tool creates a sitemap as defined by Google for your site. Enter the URL of your website(s), and the tool will generate a sitemap for you and download the compressed sitemap later. The good thing about this tool is it isn't limited to just 500 links like most of the free generators. The bad thing is it can be painfully slow and take several days to generate your free XML sitemap. There is a paid version, which (not surprisingly) is faster!

Rating: 4 Stars | **Category:** tool

GOOGLE PAGESPEED INSIGHTS - https://developers.google.com/speed/pagespeed/insights

Use this Google tool to measure how fast your website is. Size might not matter, but speed does. Google likes speedy websites! It gives you a score, plus recommendations on what you can do to speed up your website. Not just what's wrong, but what to fix. Cool tool.

Rating: 4 Stars | **Category:** tool

GOOGLE WEBMASTER CENTRAL BLOG - http://googlewebmastercentral.blogspot.com

The official blog about the Google site index, and very useful to keep up-to-date with their most recent news and new developments. It's a little geeky at times, but is especially useful with website structure issues such as naming files, robots.txt, xml sitemaps, etc.

Rating: 4 Stars | **Category:** blog

GOOGLE SEARCH CONSOLE (WEBMASTER TOOLS) HELP -
http://support.google.com/webmasters

Webmaster essentials from Google. Includes Google's official statements on SEO. To be taken with a grain of salt, because Google obviously has a huge vested interest in no one understanding how its algorithms work and thus being able to 'manipulate' search results. But here are the help files for webmasters - especially useful on webmaster issues like robots.txt, sitemaps, xml sitemaps and other 'best practices' for webmasters. Note: Google Webmaster Tools has been renamed Google Search Console.

Rating: 4 Stars | **Category:** overview

WEBMASTER CENTRAL FORUM -
https://productforums.google.com/forum/#!forum/webmasters

Google's official user forum and self-help free-for-all of webmasters helping other webmasters.

Rating: 3 Stars | **Category:** resource

GOOGLE WEBMASTERS YOUTUBE CHANNEL -
http://youtube.com/user/GoogleWebmasterHelp

This is the official YouTube channel for Google Webmasters, your one-stop shop (well, at least according to Google, but not really - but still a good place to visit...) for webmaster resources that will help you with your crawling and indexing questions, introduce you to offerings that can enhance and increase traffic to your site, and connect you with your visitors.

Rating: 3 Stars | **Category:** resource

301 REDIRECT TOOL - http://301check.com

If you reorganize your website pages, you will need to '301 redirect' the URLs for the OLD pages to URLs for the NEW pages. Use this nifty free tool to ensure they are redirected correctly.

Rating: 3 Stars | **Category:** tool

ROBOTS.TXT SYNTAX CHECKER - http://tool.motoricerca.info/robots-checker.phtml

Easy way to check your robots.txt file for valid syntax.

Rating: 3 Stars | **Category:** tool

DOMAIN INDEXING REPORT TOOL - http://seotools.com/domain-report-tool

The Domain Indexing Report Tool provides an easy way to see how your online competition measures up. The tool checks Google, Yahoo! and Bing and reports how many pages are indexed for each of the websites entered. Use this tool to find out how lightweight or heavyweight your rival sites are, so you'll know how much competitive keyword content your website needs to compete effectively.

Rating: 3 Stars | **Category:** tool

BUILTWITH - http://builtwith.com/

Useful for competitive analysis, this free tool takes a competitor website and analyzes the technologies it was 'built with.' It also highlights advertising technologies used (e.g., Google remarketing) and the hosting system they employ.

Rating: 2 Stars | **Category:** tool

.HTACCESS GENERATOR - http://www.htaccessredirect.net/

Instructions called redirects placed within a file named .htaccess on some webservers allow you to redirect one URL to another, for example jm-seo.org to www.jm-seo.org. Redirects are especially useful when moving or renaming a web page on your site. This utility will help you create the correct .htaccess file for your website, which is sometimes not straightforward.

Rating: 2 Stars | **Category:** tool

GOOGLE STRUCTURED DATA TESTING TOOL - https://developers.google.com/structured-data/testing-tool/

> With the Schema.org standard, use this tool to see if structured data you have created and inserted into your web pages is being correctly interpreted by Google.
>
> **Rating:** 2 Stars | **Category:** tool

URI VALET - https://urivalet.com/

> URI valet is another HTML / server response analysis tool. It's sort of an all-in-one tool for measuring your server response time, HTML markup, and other attributes of good HTML. Not so much an SEO tool as a best practice HTML tool.
>
> **Rating:** 2 Stars | **Category:** tool

ROBOTS.TXT GENERATOR - http://tools.seobook.com/robots-txt/generator

> A robots.txt file is simple enough, but this tool makes it even simpler. Just type in your parameters and it will create the file for you. Then copy paste it into a TXT file (using Notepad, for example), and you have your robots.txt file. You still have to upload it to your root directory, as in http://www.jm-seo.org/robots.txt.
>
> **Rating:** 1 Stars | **Category:** tool

11

LOCAL SEARCH

So much of search is local. "Dallas Roofing Company," "NYC Personal Injury Attorney," "Pizza," and so on and so forth. For many companies, therefore, going local is a big part of successful SEO. Local search crosses into *social media*, so you want your SEO to support your local search social media efforts (Get reviews!) and vice-versa. Here are the best tools and listing services for improving your local search SEO, ranked with the best tools first!

GOOGLE MY BUSINESS (GOOGLE LOCAL / GOOGLE PLACES) -
http://google.com/business

> Google My Business is the new official name, but behind-the-scenes they still call it Google Places or Google Local or Google+ Local. Or whatchamacallit. This is the official entry point to find and claim your small business listing on Google's local service.
>
> **Rating:** 5 Stars | **Category:** resource

YELP - http://biz.yelp.com

> Yelp is a local reviews service. Businesses can have (and claim) a FREE listing on Yelp, which can be helpful for local listings and local link building. This link is to the 'business' portal at Yelp - how to find, and list your business.
>
> **Rating:** 5 Stars | **Category:** service

BING PLACES FOR BUSINESS (BING LOCAL) - http://bingplaces.com

> Bing is a distant #2 to Google, behind probably Yahoo...but nonetheless, for local search purposes, it's still valuable to find (and claim) your local listing on Bing Local. So go for it, be a Binger!
>
> **Rating:** 5 Stars | **Category:** service

MOZ LOCAL - https://moz.com/local

> If local matters to you, you need to see where you're listed (Google+, Yelp, etc.), and how you're listed. You also want consistent address, phone number, and other data across local sites (called 'citations'). Moz has a new paid service for this, but this free tool will analyze (and find) your listings pretty easily.
>
> **Rating:** 5 Stars | **Category:** tool

CITYSEARCH - http://citysearch.com

> Citysearch is a local guide for better city living. It covers thousands of locations nationwide, and combines editorial recommendations, user comments, and

expert advice to keep you connected to popular and undiscovered places. It has a search tool to find businesses and services with integrated reviews. Make sure to check if you're listed and encourage good reviews.

Rating: 5 Stars | **Category:** service

INSIDER PAGES - http://insiderpages.com

Insider Pages enables people to find local businesses through recommendations from friends and neighbors. Users can create and share reviews of local businesses and perform detailed searches for businesses across the country in numerous categories.

Rating: 5 Stars | **Category:** service

GOOGLE MY BUSINESS (GOOGLE+ LOCAL / GOOGLE PLACES) HELP CENTER - https://support.google.com/business#topic=4539639

A wonderful and rather hidden microsite in the Googleplex with many help topics to learn about, modify, and update your Google+ Local listings. Google Local begot Google Places begot Google+ Local begot Google My Business. You and I both wish Google would settle on a name for its local service!

Rating: 5 Stars | **Category:** resource

SMALL BUSINESS GUIDE TO GOOGLE MY BUSINESS - http://simplybusiness.co.uk/microsites/google-my-business-guide

Interactive step-by-step flowchart to using Google My Business. Comprised of key questions and linked resources with more information. Chart is divided into different areas including setup, page management and optimization, engagement and reviews, and citations.

Rating: 4 Stars | **Category:** resource

GOOGLE PLACES CATEGORIES - http://blumenthals.com/google-lbc-categories

When setting up your free listing on Google Places, be sure to choose categories that are already existing. Use this to tool help you identify extant categories as you work on your five free categories for Google Places. Perform a search by entering a term or click the search button.

Rating: 4 Stars | **Category:** tool

LOCAL SEARCH RANKING FACTORS - http://davidmihm.com/local-search-ranking-factors.shtml

An excellent yearly survey of factors that influence local search and SEO. Scroll about half way down the page, and look at the survey / factor list. Then brainstorm ways to make your company exhibit the factors as required. Some are easy (city and state in TITLE tag), others not so much: getting closer to the city center, getting more reviews.

Rating: 4 Stars | **Category:** article

YAHOO! LOCAL - http://local.yahoo.com

Yahoo! Local is a comprehensive business directory for cities in the USA and Canada complete with ratings and reviews, maps, events, and more. Find or include your business for help not just with Yahoo but with local search on Bing and Google.

Rating: 4 Stars | **Category:** service

CITATION BUILDING STRATEGIES - THE COMPLETE LIST FOR LOCAL BUSINESSES - http://localstampede.com/citation-building-strategies-list

It's always great when someone has done the brainstorming for you. If you are a local business, local 'citations' or links are incredibly helpful.

Rating: 4 Stars | **Category:** article

GOOGLE AND YOUR BUSINESS HELP FORUM - http://productforums.google.com/forum/#!forum/business

Forums by people using Google Places, er Google and Your Business. You can get help from the community here, which is often more effective than those annoying canned emails you get from Google itself!

Rating: 4 Stars | **Category:** resource

LOCAL RANK CHECKING VIA ADWORDS - https://adwords.google.com/apt/AdPreview

This is the OFFICIAL Google AdWords preview tool. But, guess what. You can use this to vary your city location, and check your rank against various cities. If, for example, you are a pizza restaurant serving San Jose, Milpitas, and Santa Clara, you can type in 'Pizza' and see your rank in different cities. You can login to your AdWord account and click Tools - Preview Tool or use this direct link.

Rating: 4 Stars | **Category:** tool

GOOGLE MY BUSINESS (GOOGLE PLACES / GOOGLE LOCAL) HELP CENTER - https://support.google.com/business

Help with Google Places, conveniently hidden by Google..but here is where you can browse helpful articles on setting up and managing your free advertising and promotion efforts via Google Places.

Rating: 4 Stars | **Category:** resource

YELP HELP CENTER - http://www.yelp-support.com/

Here is the official Yelp help center, for both consumer and businesses. If you are new to local marketing, this is a great place to understand how it works from an official Yelp perspective. Remember, however, that what is officially presented as 'how Yelp works' isn't 100% accurate.

Rating: 4 Stars | **Category:** resource

YELP SUPPORT CENTER (FOR BUSINESS OWNERS) - http://www.yelp-support.com/Yelp_for_Business_Owners?l=en_US

Yelp's site to support both users and businesses. As a business owner, click on the links to the left, or on 'Yelp for Business Owners' card. It's better than nothing, but Yelp still has a long way to go to be easy-to-use for business owners. Easy password reset?

Rating: 4 Stars | **Category:** resource

YAHOO LOCALWORKS - https://smallbusiness.yahoo.com/localworks

Citations - mentions of your company, address, and phone number across many local listing sites - have a big impact on your rank on Google and Bing. This nifty tool from Yahoo allows you to input your business name, phone, address, and zip and get a report on where you are already indexed, and how.

Rating: 4 Stars | **Category:** service

SEO LOCAL RANKING FACTORS 2015 - https://moz.com/blog/local-search-ranking-factors-2015

Moz.com does a great job of first surveying SEO's and then compiling its best guestimate on the factors (in order) that propel a company to the top of local searches on Google.

Rating: 4 Stars | **Category:** resource

YEXT - http://www.yext.com/

Follow the instructions to 'scan your business.' This nifty tool allows you to input your business name and phone number and it will go out and find all the relevant listings across many, many different local listings services. Then you can (pay) to have it fix many of them. Not perfect, but a good start on identifying logical local listing opportunities for your business.

Rating: 4 Stars | **Category:** tool

GOOGLE STRUCTURED DATA MARKUP HELPER - https://google.com/webmasters/markup-helper

Structured data, or microdata, allows Google and other search engines to know if you have an event with dates, a picture you want as your logo, or even a recipe calorie count. Very useful for local search optimization. Use this free tool to generate the required markup.

Rating: 4 Stars | **Category:** tool

GOOGLE+ PAGE SEARCH - http://www.gpluspagesearch.com/

Use this nifty site to find competitor Google+ pages easily. Just enter a competitor name (or your own business name), and this search engine will identify the relevant Google+ page.

Rating: 4 Stars | **Category:** tool

BEST LOCAL CITATIONS BY CATEGORY - http://moz.com/learn/local/citations-by-category

If you're 'into local,' then you gotta know your citation sources. Obviously, Google+ is the most important for Google, and in many markets Yelp is #2. But for a plumber vs. a chiropractor, where to get citations (listings on local sites) can be different. Moz breaks out the 'best' citation sources by common category.

Rating: 4 Stars | **Category:** article

LOCAL KEYWORD LIST GENERATOR - http://5minutesite.com/local_keywords.php

Don't know your local geography? What about all those pesky zip codes and small suburban towns? Enter a zip code or city into this tool, and it generates a nifty list of possible nearby locales and zips for your SEO efforts. A time saver if local search is important to your SEO.

Rating: 3 Stars | **Category:** tool

BRIGHTLOCAL REVIEWBIZ WIDGET - http://brightlocal.com/seo-tools/review-biz

Technically not a free tool, but getting reviews is so important, and this little widget makes an all-in-one how to ask for a review widget.

Rating: 3 Stars | **Category:** tool

YELP BLOG FOR BUSINESS OWNERS - https://biz.yelp.com/blog

If local SEO / local SMM / Yelp matters to you, well, you MUST subscribe to and follow the official Yelp blog. Take it all with a grain of salt and a good dose of skepticism, as it is the OFFICIAL blog, so it gives you a good dose of Yelp-is-so-fantastic propaganda, but it is the official source.

Rating: 3 Stars | **Category:** blog

LocalVox - http://localvox.com/free-report

Find out if, and where, your local business is listed. Then go and get listed!

Rating: 3 Stars | **Category:** service

Microformats Code & Tools - http://microformats.org/wiki/code-tools

Microdata, rich snippets, microformats - whatever you call them they are important! For local search, you want to 'tell' Google / Bing your location. This page gives you the ability to generate that code for your webpages, free.

Rating: 3 Stars | **Category:** tool

Schema.org 'Local' Schema Creator - http://51blocks.com/checklists-tools/schema-creator

If you are a local business and easily can add HTML code to your site, you can use this tool to generate structured data to enable search engines to better 'understand' you.

Rating: 3 Stars | **Category:** tool

Ultimate Guide to Microformats: Reference and Examples - http://sixrevisions.com/web-development/ultimate-guide-to-microformats-reference-and-examples

Microdata, rich snippets, microformats - whatever you call them they are important. If you aren't familiar with microformats, this article is a great introduction.

Rating: 3 Stars | **Category:** article

GOOGLE REVIEW HANDOUT GENERATOR - http://whitespark.ca/review-handout-generator

This very slick tool allows you to input your company, website, and logo and then it generates a very nice-looking PDF / handout you can give your clients and thereby solicit Google reviews. The PDF is very well done.

Rating: 3 Stars | **Category:** tool

YELP ADVERTISER FAQ - http://yelp.com/advertiser_faq

Many business owners hate Yelp. In fact, hate might be a mild word. Here is Yelp's side of the story, responding to criticism of their review system. Take it with a grain of salt: it is Yelp's side of the story, but it has interesting factoids in it, such as how incredibly powerful negative reviews can affect your business.

Rating: 2 Stars | **Category:** article

EXTENDING HTML5 — MICROFORMATS - http://html5doctor.com/microformats/

If you're anything like my amazing 20 year old daughter, you have no idea what microformats are. Well, never fear, HTML5 Doctor has you covered. This article is an extensive introduction into microformats and provides everything you need to know (and more).

Rating: 2 Stars | **Category:** article

GEOSITEMAPGENERATOR - http://geositemapgenerator.com

This doesn't really generate a sitemap. Rather it tells Google and Bing your physical address, which is a useful signal for local SEO.

Rating: 1 Stars | **Category:** tool

YELP WEBINARS FOR BUSINESS - https://biz.yelp.com/blog/upcoming-webinar-schedule-2

Yelp produces OFFICIAL webinars not only on Yelp advertising but on how to create a good free listing. All of this with the caveat that they only tell you the official stuff, not the secret tips and tricks, but still worth while.

Rating: 1 Stars | **Category:** blog

12

GOOGLE+

Google+ is the new (troubled) kid on the social media block, and this new kid has a powerful daddy: Google. Google+ is currently under much reconstruction. However, it has a huge impact on local search results. So if local matters to you, so does Google+.

Here are the best **free** Google+ tools on the Internet, ranked with the best tools first!

GOOGLE MY BUSINESS (GOOGLE LOCAL / GOOGLE PLACES) -
http://google.com/business

> Google My Business is the new official name, but behind-the-scenes they still call it Google Places or Google Local or Google+ Local. Or whatchamacallit. This is the official entry point to find and claim your small business listing on Google's local service.
>
> **Rating:** 5 Stars | **Category:** resource

GOOGLE MY BUSINESS (GOOGLE+ LOCAL / GOOGLE PLACES) HELP CENTER -
https://support.google.com/business#topic=4539639

> A wonderful and rather hidden microsite in the Googleplex with many help topics to learn about, modify, and update your Google+ Local listings. Google Local begot Google Places begot Google+ Local begot Google My Business. You and I both wish Google would settle on a name for its local service!
>
> **Rating:** 5 Stars | **Category:** resource

SMALL BUSINESS GUIDE TO GOOGLE+ -
http://simplybusiness.co.uk/microsites/googleplus-for-small-businesses

> Interactive step-by-step flowchart to using Google+ for small business. Comprised of key questions and linked resources with more information. Chart is divided into different areas including set up, integration, and engagement. Worth a look.
>
> **Rating:** 4 Stars | **Category:** resource

GOOGLE+ AUTO AWESOME - https://support.google.com/plus/topic/6034292

> If Google+ has excelled anywhere, it's photos. Did you know that hidden inside Google+ is a photo editing tool named Auto Awesome? Well, this introduction will teach you how to use it to add effects to your photos and videos.
>
> **Rating:** 4 Stars | **Category:** tool

GOOGLE+ PLATFORM - https://developers.google.com/+

Here is the nifty, geeky developers site with all the code used for Google+ features.

Rating: 4 Stars | **Category:** resource

GOOGLE+ +1 BUTTON - https://developers.google.com/+/web/+1button

The Google+ +1 button allows users to 'vote' that your page is cool and important, and they can share it across Google+. This document is intended for webmasters and programmers who want to add and customize the +1 button for their website. Customizations range from simply changing the button's size to advanced loading techniques.

Rating: 4 Stars | **Category:** service

GOOGLE+ BADGE - https://developers.google.com/+/web/badge

This page explains how to add a Google+ badge to your website. Similar, we think, to the Facebook Like button or Like box, this feature will allow users to directly add your page to their Google+ account.

Rating: 4 Stars | **Category:** service

GOOGLE+ PAGE SEARCH - http://www.gpluspagesearch.com/

Use this nifty site to find competitor Google+ pages easily. Just enter a competitor name (or your own business name), and this search engine will identify the relevant Google+ page.

Rating: 4 Stars | **Category:** tool

OFFICIAL GOOGLE SOCIAL MEDIA - http://google.com/press/google-directory.html

Does Google use Social Media? Of course, it does. Whatever Google product you are into (SEO, AdWords, G+), you can identify the blog, the YouTube channel, the Twitter, etc., of your Google product. Follow Google on social media.

Rating: 4 Stars | **Category:** resource

NOD3x - http://nod3x.com

NOD3x is a real-time, social network analysis and data mining application. It provides insights for all major social networks, though the free version only does so for Google+. It can track and index all posts about any subject made to a personal profile or Google+ page timeline and/or public community. From there it offers all manner of statistics on posts, influencers, gender, keywords, location, sentiment, etc.

Rating: 3 Stars | **Category:** tool

ULTIMATE GOOGLE+ QUICKSTARTER GUIDE - http://martinshervington.com/the-ultimate-google-plus-quickstarter-guide

If you'd like to come up to speed on Google+ and prefer someone show you, step-by-step, then this video tutorial & resource guide is a great starting point. The accompanying text includes links to pages, each dedicated to various Google+ features, complete with additional video and tips.

Rating: 3 Stars | **Category:** tutorial

CIRCLECOUNT - http://www.circlecount.com/

Interesting statistical tool which analyzes your Google+ Profile and Pages in addition to providing a wealth of general Google+ usage information including users with highly engaging content, most followed profiles, most followed pages, to name just a few.

Rating: 3 Stars | **Category:** tool

GOOGLE+ HANGOUTS - http://gphangouts.com

Hangouts on Google+ are video and text chat rooms. Corporations and individuals can use them to encourage potential customers or fans to 'hangout' and talk with each other, and with you. Great service to identify Google+ hangouts and even create your own.

Rating: 3 Stars | **Category:** service

GOOGLE+ DEVELOPERS BLOG - http://googleplusplatform.blogspot.com

A little geeky, but this is the official blog for people who are developing for Google+.

Rating: 3 Stars | **Category:** blog

GOOGLE+ VIDEO TUTORIALS - http://slideshare.net/martinsherv/google-tutorials-17140683

This short presentation is chock full of links to YouTube videos on all aspects of Google+, including an extensive section on Google+ for Business.

Rating: 3 Stars | **Category:** tutorial

GOOGLE+ UNIVERSITY - A COMPLETE CURRICULUM FOR BUSINESS - http://thesmh.co/GooglePlusU

These free lessons are designed for you to create a successful Google+ presence for your business. It consists of six 'courses', each comprised of several chapters, intended to take learners from Beginner (101) all the way to Advanced (601). Content will be updated over time to meet the needs of this evolving portion of the social media landscape.

Rating: 3 Stars | **Category:** resource

GOOGLE+ WIDGET - http://widgetsplus.com

Are you, or your company, REALLY active on Google+? This nifty widget will stream your posts to your web page or blog, allowing users to see your posts and hopefully decide to follow you on Google+.

Rating: 3 Stars | **Category:** tool

GOOGLE+: HOW TO LEARN IT IN 6 WEEKS, FREE OF CHARGE - http://slideshare.net/martinsherv/free-google-6-week-course

This extensive, completely free, and largely video-based Google+ training course makes learning easy by using a layered approach. Namely, the content in is organized in logical chunks which builds upon itself. Also includes links to many resources.

Rating: 3 Stars | **Category:** tutorial

ALL MY + STATISTICS - http://allmyplus.com

This third-party tool helps you analyze what, if anything, is going on in your Google+ account. Make the stark interface more understandable by clicking the 'more info' links to display helpful explanations for each function.

Rating: 3 Stars | **Category:** tool

WHAT THE PLUS!: GOOGLE+ FOR THE REST OF US - http://www.tradepub.com/free/w_guyk01

Author, speaker, entrepreneur, evangelist and social media phenomenon Guy Kawasaki thought highly enough of Google+ to write a book about it. Click the button to download the ebook version free.

Rating: 3 Stars | **Category:** book

CIRCLOSCOPE - https://chrome.google.com/webstore/detail/circloscope/mechgkelogghhgmpmbpofjijifdppppl

Circloscope is an advanced Google+ Circles management tool available only as a Chrome extension. With it you can do things like find the most followed people in your circles, the relevant people in your circles, Google+ users in your contacts, and much more. Free and premium plans are available.

Rating: 3 Stars | **Category:** tool

CHROME DO SHARE - https://chrome.google.com/webstore/detail/do-share/oglhhmnmdocfhmhlekfdecokagmbchnf

Allows you to schedule posts to personal profiles on Google+, something not easily done with other plugins or applications.

Rating: 3 Stars | **Category:** tool

FRIENDS+ME - https://friendsplus.me

This nifty tool allows you to share your Google+ post to other social networks such as Facebook or Twitter.

Rating: 3 Stars | **Category:** tool

GET AN A+ ON G+: HELPING YOU MAKE THE GRADE ON G+ - https://plus.google.com/+KristofferHowes/posts/7G4YYAoHdwZ

In a novel (no pun intended) approach to publishing, this helpful book is about Google+ is written and available only on Google+. Its content, divided into preface, 5 chapters, and afterthoughts, consists solely of Google+ blog posts, each of which is described and linked here.

Rating: 3 Stars | **Category:** book

GOOGLE+ EXPLORE - https://plus.google.com/explore

Monitor the most popular Google+ content for blog post ideas using the Explore feature. Surprisingly easy to use interface and infinite scrolling makes searching and browsing a breeze. Try it today.

Rating: 3 Stars | **Category:** resource

GOOGLE+ SEARCH - https://plus.google.com/people/find

Beyond just searching plus.google.com, you can use this feature 'inside' of Google+ to find people, pages and posts that might be interesting. Curious how hard Google has made Google+ to search, isn't it? That's just weird, but this is how you can search for people on G+.

Rating: 3 Stars | **Category:** tool

GOOGLE PLUS - FREQUENTLY ASKED QUESTIONS! -
https://plusyourbusiness.com/google-plus-frequently-asked-questions

> For those just getting started with Google+, this FAQ does a surprisingly good job decoding its jargon and shedding light on some of its idiosyncrasies.
>
> **Rating:** 3 Stars | **Category:** resource

STEADY DEMAND - https://steadydemand.com

> Steady Demand provides free analysis of your Google+ page. Enter your Google+ page ID (e.g., +Jm-seoOrg) and receive a report consisting of Google+ Page analysis and Post analysis. Page analysis assesses your page on about 6 criteria, while the Post analysis presents some aggregate statistics along with a detailed assessment of your last 10 posts. Helpful but not earth shattering.
>
> **Rating:** 3 Stars | **Category:** tool

GOOGLE+ INSIGHTS - https://support.google.com/business/answer/4570078

> Understand the effectiveness of your business' Google+ Page with Google+ Insights, a lightweight analytics tool by Google for Google My Business page owners. The tool is accessible from your My Business home page and provides data via three sections: Visibility (number of cumulative views of your page), Engagement (actions, i.e., +1s, shares, comments your content has received), and Audience (number of new followers of your local Google+ page). Insights is also available via the Google My Business mobile app.
>
> **Rating:** 3 Stars | **Category:** service

GOOGLE+ HELP CENTER - https://support.google.com/plus

> Already lost? Here is the official Google+ support pages, focused mainly on users of Google+. But, as a business, these help pages give good insights into how your customer might use Google+. Make sure to be a user of Google+ as well as a producer - and here's where you go to learn how to use Google+.
>
> **Rating:** 3 Stars | **Category:** resource

GOOGLE+ RECOMMENDED USERS - http://www.recommendedusers.com/

Think no one is on Google+? That there's nothing fun under the sun? Think again. Use this site to find the cool, fun, cognoscenti in the world of Google+.

Rating: 3 Stars | **Category:** resource

GPLUS.TO - GOOGLE PLUS URL SHORTENER - http://gplus.to

Need a nifty short Google-looking URL for your Google+ account? This service - not affiliated with Google+ - may be your answer.

Rating: 1 Stars | **Category:** service

13

GOOGLE

Throughout this *Toolbook*, we have mentioned many official Google resources. Google produces a cornucopia of free tools and resources for the SEO aficionado. Here, in this chapter, we bring them all under one roof: everything free by Google, about Google.

Here are the best **free** official Google tools on the Internet, ranked with the best tools first!

GOOGLE SEARCH CONSOLE (WEBMASTER TOOLS) -
https://www.google.com/webmasters/

Google Webmaster Tools provides detailed reports about your pages' visibility on Google. To get started, simply add and verify your site and begin seeing information right away. Get Google's view of your site and diagnose problems. See how Google crawls and indexes your site and learn about specific problems they're having accessing it. Discover your link and query traffic. Also contains an extensive education section with videos and articles to help you get found on Google.

Rating: 5 Stars | **Category:** tool

GOOGLE SEO STARTER GUIDE - http://bit.ly/google-seo-starter

This is the one, and only, really good resource by Google that is an official guide to what to do when, how, where and why for SEO. It covers mainly 'on page' SEO but definitely identifies basic tasks to accomplish on your website. Highly recommended.

Rating: 5 Stars | **Category:** resource

GOOGLE ANALYTICS - http://google.com/analytics

Google Analytics is an enterprise-class web analytics solution which provides detailed insights into your website traffic and marketing effectiveness. Powerful features let you see and analyze your traffic data to be more prepared to write better-targeted ads, strengthen marketing initiatives and create higher converting websites.

Rating: 5 Stars | **Category:** tool

GOOGLE MY BUSINESS (GOOGLE LOCAL / GOOGLE PLACES) -
http://google.com/business

Google My Business is the new official name, but behind-the-scenes they still call it Google Places or Google Local or Google+ Local. Or whatchamacallit. This is the official entry point to find and claim your small business listing on Google's local service.

Rating: 5 Stars | **Category:** resource

GOOGLE SUPPORT CENTER - https://support.google.com/

The ULTIMATE place to find Google help. It's kind of hidden in the Googleplex, but this is the master Google support center. Type any Google-related question into the search box and simultaneously search YouTube, AdWords, Analytics, and all Google products for answers. You got questions? Here are the answers to everything Google-related.

Rating: 5 Stars | **Category:** resource

GOOGLE WEBMASTER ACADEMY - http://support.google.com/webmasters/answer/6001102

Google's learning site for SEO. Basic stuff, and a bit salesy, but a good starting point. Just remember who's talking - Google - and take it all with a grain of salt.

Rating: 5 Stars | **Category:** resource

GOOGLE WEBMASTERS YOUTUBE CHANNEL - http://youtube.com/googlewebmasterhelp

If you are a webmaster or someone interested in search engine optimization, this is a great site of YouTube videos created by Google. Of course it is the 'party line' from the biggest player in search - dare we say, the view of the search monopolist on what constitutes acceptable behavior? Especially useful on technical website structure issues.

Rating: 4 Stars | **Category:** video

GOOGLE ANALYTICS BLOG - http://analytics.blogspot.com

Official blog by Google Analytics Team. The horse's mouth, as it were. Pay attention to the 'back to basics' tag. This blog is more for professional, really serious Google Analytics folks. That said, you can search the blog and find some interesting content.

Rating: 4 Stars | **Category:** blog

GOOGLE EMAIL ALERTS - http://google.com/alerts

Use Google to alert you by email for search results that matter to you. Input your company name, for example, to see when new web pages, blog posts, or other items surface on the web. Enter your target keywords to keep an eye on yourself and your competitors. Part of the Gmail system.

Rating: 4 Stars | **Category:** service

OFFICIAL GOOGLE SOCIAL MEDIA - http://google.com/press/google-directory.html

Does Google use Social Media? Of course, it does. Whatever Google product you are into (SEO, AdWords, G+), you can identify the blog, the YouTube channel, the Twitter, etc., of your Google product. Follow Google on social media.

Rating: 4 Stars | **Category:** resource

GOOGLE WEBMASTER CENTRAL BLOG - http://googlewebmastercentral.blogspot.com

The official blog about the Google site index, and very useful to keep up-to-date with their most recent news and new developments. It's a little geeky at times, but is especially useful with website structure issues such as naming files, robots.txt, xml sitemaps, etc.

Rating: 4 Stars | **Category:** blog

GOOGLE SEARCH CONSOLE (WEBMASTER TOOLS) HELP - http://support.google.com/webmasters

Webmaster essentials from Google. Includes Google's official statements on SEO. To be taken with a grain of salt, because Google obviously has a huge vested interest in no one understanding how its algorithms work and thus being able to 'manipulate' search results. But here are the help files for webmasters - especially useful on webmaster issues like robots.txt, sitemaps, xml sitemaps and other 'best practices' for webmasters. Note: Google Webmaster Tools has been renamed Google Search Console.

Rating: 4 Stars | **Category:** overview

GOOGLE INSIDE ADWORDS BLOG - http://adwords.blogspot.com

The official blog for Google AdWords. It's more for sophisticated users than for newbies, but - that said - you should pay attention to it if you are spending money with Google.

Rating: 4 Stars | **Category:** blog

GOOGLE ANALYTICS YOUTUBE CHANNEL - http://youtube.com/googleanalytics

Official YouTube channel for Google Analytics. In conjunction with Google's Conversion University, this YouTube channel has a wealth of information on Google's web analytics and online advertising products in easy-to-use video format. Ideally, Google channels on YouTube would be centralized, but if you pay attention to this channel as well as Google My Business, you have the primary Google venues covered.

Rating: 4 Stars | **Category:** video

ASK GOOGLE - https://varvy.com/search.html

Ask Google is a way to query OFFICIAL Google websites, such as the Webmaster Tools blog or Google's mega support site - support.google.com. They are using Google custom search to build this, but it's a nifty and useful way to find the official Google help files on any topic of interest to you in SEO.

Rating: 4 Stars | **Category:** tool

GOOGLE PRODUCT FORUMS - GET USER HELP - https://productforums.google.com/forum/#!home

This is the MASTER link for ALL of the Google product forums, such as AdWords, Analytics, Webmaster Tools, etc., wherein users help users and, if lucky, official Googlers chime in with helpful hints, tips, tricks and secrets about individual Google products.

Rating: 4 Stars | **Category:** resource

GOOGLE SEARCH OPERATORS -
https://support.google.com/websearch/answer/2466433

You can use Google search in special ways for your SEO strategy. One is to use the syntax site:yourcompany.com to find out how many pages are already in the Google index. Another is to use the phrase related:domain.com to find pages 'similar' to a page. Type related:nytimes.com to find sites that are 'similar' to the New York Times. Finally, use the ~ (tilde) character to ask Google for synonyms. ~CPR will give you first aid, for example.

Rating: 3 Stars | **Category:** overview

THINK WITH GOOGLE - https://www.thinkwithgoogle.com/

This flashy, very Madison Avenue ad agency guide is a gateway to fun and sometime informative studies by Google about Google, and about Internet advertising and marketing in general. It pushes AdWords, of course, but still has a wealth of fun stuff about Internet marketing.

Rating: 3 Stars | **Category:** resource

GOOGLE DRIVE - http://drive.google.com

If you have a Google account, you already have access to 'Google Drive.' Google Drive is Google's FREE cloud drive - you can upload documents, spreadsheets, even notes and then share these. You can even create surveys for customers on Google Drive.

Rating: 3 Stars | **Category:** service

GOOGLE ADVANCED SEARCH - https://www.google.com/advanced_search

If you don't know all those esoteric Google search operators, use Google Advanced Search. As any smart small business marketer will tell you, competitive intelligence is very important. So use advanced search to do 'market research' on your industry, including keyword targets for SEO.

Rating: 3 Stars | **Category:** tool

GOOGLE ON FACEBOOK - https://www.facebook.com/Google

Google's official page on Facebook. Do you like Google? Like Google on Facebook.

Rating: 3 Stars | **Category:** resource

GOOGLE YOUTUBE CHANNELS DIRECTORY - http://www.google.com/press/youtube-directory.html

Directory of official YouTube channels by Google, about Google.

Rating: 3 Stars | **Category:** resource

GOOGLE DASHBOARD - http://google.com/settings/dashboard

Want to see and manage all Google properties associated with your Google Account? Visit Google Dashboard. It's a comprehensive list and includes everything from contacts you're storing, to alerts set up, to uploaded YouTube videos. Worth bookmarking.

Rating: 3 Stars | **Category:** resource

GOOGLE WEB & APP ACTIVITY - https://history.google.com/history/

Prepare to be creeped out. If you are SIGNED IN to your Google account, and click on this link, you'll see a HISTORY of EVERYTHING you have searched for, if you haven't disabled this. Remember privacy? Oops, that is soooo 1999. You can 'delete' your history but then again, can you trust that Google really, really deletes it?

Rating: 3 Stars | **Category:** service

GOOGLE HELP FORUMS - https://productforums.google.com/forum/#!home;lang=en

Got a questions? Perhaps someone else who cares about Google has an answer. Use these online forums to post questions and get answers from the Google web community. Has threads on AdWords, Webmaster Tools, Blogs and more!

Rating: 3 Stars | **Category:** newsgroup

GOOGLE BLOG DIRECTORY - http://www.google.com/press/blog-directory.html

An incomplete(!) list of Google's own blogs. These are blogs by Google about Google's products. Some blogs do not seem to be here - such as Matt Cutt's personal blog or even the Google Analytics blogs - or you really have to hunt to find them. But it is a starting point if you think that there 'should' be a blog by Google about a Google product or service.

Rating: 3 Stars | **Category:** resource

WEBMASTER CENTRAL FORUM - https://productforums.google.com/forum/#!forum/webmasters

Google's official user forum and self-help free-for-all of webmasters helping other webmasters.

Rating: 3 Stars | **Category:** resource

GOOGLE ALGORITHM CHANGE HISTORY - https://moz.com/google-algorithm-change

For history buffs, the Google algorithm change history from Moz should prove interesting reading. If you're an analytics nerd and can't figure out why your page hits suddenly dropped without explanation, the dates of these Google updates might provide an Aha! moment.

Rating: 3 Stars | **Category:** resource

GOOGLE YOUTUBE CHANNEL - https://www.youtube.com/Google

The official Google channel on YouTube, oriented mainly at consumers and full of Google ads.

Rating: 3 Stars | **Category:** resource

GOOGLE BLOG (OFFICIAL) - https://googleblog.blogspot.com/

This is the official Google 'corporate' blog. This has anything and everything about Google by Google, but is really a corporate marketing vehicle. In most cases, webmasters and SEO people will need to look deeper at the more nuanced blogs on the blogosphere by Google on Google for help and issues.

Rating: 3 Stars | **Category:** blog

GOOGLE GET YOUR BUSINESS ONLINE - http://gybo.com

Google will literally give you a website if you do not have one as a small business. For one year, you can get a free Google website. So now there really is no excuse not to have a website!

Rating: 2 Stars | **Category:** resource

GOOGLE TAKEOUT - https://www.google.com/settings/takeout

If you are a frequent user of Google tools, such as Google Docs, this nifty application allows you to download a copy of your data stored withing Google products, thereby retaining all your stuff.

Rating: 2 Stars | **Category:** tool

GOOGLE TWITTER DIRECTORY - http://google.com/press/twitter-directory.html

Can't get enough Google? Don't forget about Google on Twitter. Here is a directory of all the Google outposts on Twitter.

Rating: 2 Stars | **Category:** misc.

GOOGLE YOUTUBE CHANNELS DIRECTORY - https://www.google.com/press/youtube-directory.html

Directory of all the official Google channels on YouTube. So if you want to find out if Google Analytics has an official YouTube channel, this is a good place to start.

Rating: 1 Stars | **Category:** resource

14

METRICS

Google Analytics is the best free Web metrics tool available today. But what should you measure? What information can you get out of your website that you can feed back into your SEO strategy for further improvement? The first step is to figure out what you want to measure. Second is to set up a basic Google Analytics account. Third is to use advanced Analytics to "slice and dice" your data to obtain data you can really use. Beyond Google, there are other great metrics tools out there as well.

Here are the best **free** metrics tools on the Internet, ranked with the best tools first!

GOOGLE ANALYTICS - http://google.com/analytics

Google Analytics is an enterprise-class web analytics solution which provides detailed insights into your website traffic and marketing effectiveness. Powerful features let you see and analyze your traffic data to be more prepared to write better-targeted ads, strengthen marketing initiatives and create higher converting websites.

Rating: 5 Stars | **Category:** tool

GOOGLE ANALYTICS ACADEMY - https://analyticsacademy.withgoogle.com

If you are using Google Analytics, this is a must-see treasure trove of information on how to use that powerful platform. Ironically, it can be very difficult to jump from Google Analytics over to the Google Analytics Training and Certification site. Only Google knows why they made it so difficult. That said, check out the topics and videos here. If you are serious, you can study and become qualified as an Analytics Expert!

Rating: 5 Stars | **Category:** tutorial

GOOGLE ANALYTICS TRAINING RESOURCES -
http://support.google.com/analytics/answer/4553001

Another gateway to the wonderful world of Google Analytics training and learning. It has a set up checklist, links to seminars and videos, as well as the Analytics and Academy IQ learning centers. A MUST VISIT site if you are interested in mastering Google Analytics and gaining certification.

Rating: 5 Stars | **Category:** resource

GOOGLE ANALYTICS SOLUTIONS GALLERY -
https://www.google.com/analytics/gallery/#landing/start/

Here are some pre-formatted reports, Advanced Segments, and other goodies that Google has collected from its community for small business users. Rather than re-invent the wheel, browse the Gallery to find an example of what you need. Then quickly import it into your own Google Analytics account.

Rating: 4 Stars | **Category:** resource

GOOGLE ANALYTICS CAMPAIGNS URL BUILDER -
https://support.google.com/analytics/answer/1033867

Use this tool to build URLs to track your ad campaigns. For instance, if you have ad campaigns on Facebook or LinkedIn, you can use this tool from Google to make them easier to track in Google Analytics.

Rating: 4 Stars | **Category:** tool

GOOGLE ANALYTICS APPS - http://google.com/analytics/apps

This gallery contains applications that extend Google Analytics in new and exciting ways. They are solutions that help analysts, marketers, IT teams, and executives get more out of Google Analytics.

Rating: 4 Stars | **Category:** tool

GOOGLE ANALYTICS YOUTUBE CHANNEL - http://youtube.com/googleanalytics

Official YouTube channel for Google Analytics. In conjunction with Google's Conversion University, this YouTube channel has a wealth of information on Google's web analytics and online advertising products in easy-to-use video format. Ideally, Google channels on YouTube would be centralized, but if you pay attention to this channel as well as Google My Business, you have the primary Google venues covered.

Rating: 4 Stars | **Category:** video

GOOGLE SEARCH CONSOLE (WEBMASTER TOOLS) -
https://www.google.com/webmasters/

Google Webmaster Tools provides detailed reports about your pages' visibility on Google. To get started, simply add and verify your site and begin seeing information right away. Get Google's view of your site and diagnose problems. See how Google crawls and indexes your site and learn about specific problems they're having accessing it. Discover your link and query traffic. Also contains an extensive education section with videos and articles to help you get found on Google.

Rating: 5 Stars | **Category:** tool

PIWIK - http://piwik.org

Does Google knowing everything, including your site Analytics, give you the creeps? Then fight the power with Piwik, an open source analytics platform that allows you to own your data. Download the self-hosted version for free or pay for the hosted service. Piwik provides all the web analytics features you'd expect, including a customizable dashboard, goal conversion tracking, and a wide-variety of predefined reports.

Rating: 4 Stars | **Category:** service

SMALL BUSINESS GUIDE TO GOOGLE ANALYTICS - http://simplybusiness.co.uk/microsites/google-analytics-guide

Interactive step-by-step flowchart to using Google Analytics more effectively. Comprised of key questions and linked resources with more information. Definitely worth a look if Google Analytics has you stumped.

Rating: 4 Stars | **Category:** resource

GOOGLE ANALYTICS BLOG - http://analytics.blogspot.com

Official blog by Google Analytics Team. The horse's mouth, as it were. Pay attention to the 'back to basics' tag. This blog is more for professional, really serious Google Analytics folks. That said, you can search the blog and find some interesting content.

Rating: 4 Stars | **Category:** blog

GOOGLE ANALYTICS HELP CENTER - http://support.google.com/analytics

'High level' site of all the support and help options for Google Analytics. Most are covered elsewhere, but they do have an official partner network. So it's a good place to start if you want to hire an analytics consultant.

Rating: 4 Stars | **Category:** resource

GOOGLE ANALYTICS TEST - http://www.googleanalyticstest.com/

Are you go-go for Google Analytics? Do you like punishment? Want to rekindle fond memories of multiple choice hell from High School? If so, this resource is for you. It's a deep dive into Google Analytics in preparation for taking the Google Analytics qualifying exam. If you like punishment, or just Google Analytics, this is the go-to learning site for you.

Rating: 3 Stars | **Category:** resource

GOOGLE ANALYTICS PRODUCT FORUM - http://bit.ly/adw-ganal

This is the official Google Analytics product forum, wherein users can post questions and get answers from other Google Analytics users as well as official Googlers. Unfortunately, it is clearly now part of AdWords, so everything is a bit tilted towards the needs of AdWords (and Google's bottom line).

Rating: 3 Stars | **Category:** resource

GOOGLE ANALYTICS ON FACEBOOK - http://facebook.com/GoogleAnalytics

Do you like Google Analytics? Really, really like Google Analytics? Then 'Like' Google Analytics on Facebook for all the fun that is, and can be, a good metric stroll down the lane in Google Analytics.

Rating: 3 Stars | **Category:** resource

GA (GOOGLE ANALYTICS) CHECKER - http://www.gachecker.com/

Once you sign up for Google Analytics, the tracking code must be included on EACH and EVERY page you wish to track. This nifty tool crawls your entire site, and gives you a report of pages that DO NOT have the tracking code.

Rating: 3 Stars | **Category:** tool

GOOGLE ANALYTICS ON GOOGLE+ - https://plus.google.com/+GoogleAnalytics

Official Google Analytics page on the Google+ network.

Rating: 3 Stars | **Category:** resource

GOOGLE ANALYTICS ON TWITTER - https://twitter.com/googleanalytics

Follow every tweet, every twist, every turn of metrics and analytics by following your friends at Google Analytics on their official Twitter profile.

Rating: 3 Stars | **Category:** resource

GOOGLE ANALYTICS PARTNERS APPS - https://www.google.com/analytics/partners/search/apps

Marketplace containing widgets, apps, and offerings from Google and other experts in the Google Analytics area. Useful if you want to 'outsource' some of your Google Analytics functions.

Rating: 3 Stars | **Category:** resource

GOOGLE ANALYTICS ALTERNATIVES - http://www.adpushup.com/blog/web-analytics-tools-google-analytics-alternatives/

Can't, or won't, or don't want to use Google Analytics? What - you think that privacy should still exist as a concept in society? Oops, we're calling the Google thought police right now. Before they show up to look you away, consider this article with pointers to non-Google metrics resources. You can use non-Google tools to measure what happens on your website. But why would you want to? Wink, wink. 2+2=5.

Rating: 3 Stars | **Category:** resource

WORDPRESS ANALYTICS PLUGIN - https://yoast.com/wordpress/plugins/google-analytics/

From the folks you brought you Yoast, they bring you Google Analytics for WordPress. If you're running WordPress, this is a 'must install.'

Rating: 2 Stars | **Category:** tool

GOOGLE ANALYTICS DEVELOPERS - https://developers.google.com/analytics

If you are a programmer or have one who works for you, this is the 'go to' resource for hard core programming resources on Google Analytics. Not really for mere mortals, however.

Rating: 1 Stars | **Category:** resource

15

MEDIA

Google, Google, Google. For many webmasters and web surfers, it's Google 24/7. But for the busy small business owner or marketer, how can you keep up with all the changes in SEO? It's not easy, but fortunately there are a few really good publications and conferences on search engine optimization. Beyond the official Google blogs and sites, here are third party blogs and publications on SEO.

Here are the best **free** media sites on SEO, ranked in priority order.

SEARCH ENGINE LAND - http://searchengineland.com/

Search Engine Land is a news and information site covering search engine marketing, searching issues and the search engine industry and is led by journalist Danny Sullivan, one of the world's foremost search experts.

Rating: 5 Stars | **Category:** portal

SEARCH ENGINE WATCH - http://searchenginewatch.com/

Search Engine Watch provides tips and information about searching the web, analysis of the search engine industry and help to site owners trying to improve their ability to be found in search engines. One of the leading websites for those in the SEO industry.

Rating: 5 Stars | **Category:** portal

SEARCH ENGINE ROUNDTABLE - https://www.seroundtable.com/

Search Engine Roundtable reports on the most interesting threads taking place at the SEM (Search Engine Marketing) forums. By enlisting some of the most recognized names at those forums, the Roundtable is able to report on these outstanding threads and provide a synopsis that provides greater detail into those threads.

Rating: 3 Stars | **Category:** portal

SEARCH ENGINE JOURNAL - http://www.searchenginejournal.com/

Search Engine Journal helps marketers succeed by producing best-in-industry guides and information while cultivating a positive community. It covers the marketing world daily with breaking news, in-depth subject guides, market information with perspective, argumentative and observational posts by expert guest contributors, infographics, videos, interviews, and more.

Rating: 3 Stars | **Category:** blog

SEARCH ENGINE GUIDE - http://www.searchengineguide.com/

Search Engine Guide is another 'definitive' guide to search engine information on the Internet. It's an educational website aimed at translating the search marketing world into something small business owners can understand, and is divided into four primary areas: Search Engine News, Search Engine Marketing, Internet Search Engines, and Search Engine Books & Services.

Rating: 3 Stars | **Category:** blog

MOZ BLOG - http://seomoz.org/blog

Moz (formerly SEOMoz) is the leading source on SEO by nerds for nerds. It's a bit hard to digest as much of it is 'nerdspeak.' But, that said, these people really know their stuff, and if you are serious about staying informed on SEO, follow these guys.

Rating: 3 Stars | **Category:** blog

CONFERENCES

It's funny. SEO is all about the Internet, and Google is nothing if not a virtual company. Yet there are real-world trade shows / conferences where carbon-based life forms (*that would be you and me*), go to meet and greet. If you have a budget, attending an SEO conference can be a great investment, especially after you've mastered the basics.

Here are the best **trade shows** or **conferences** on Search Engine Optimization.

Search Marketing Expo (SMX) - http://searchmarketingexpo.com

Search Marketing Expo, or SMX, is the search engine marketing conference from Third Door Media, the company behind the Search Engine Land news site, and the Search Marketing Now webcast series. SMX is programmed by the sharpest minds in search marketing.

Rating: 4 Stars | **Category:** conference

SES Conference - http://sesconference.com

SES is a leading global event series about search and social marketing. Focusing on tactics and best practices, SES events bring together thought leaders and industry experts, from private consultants to representatives from the search engines themselves, to provide YOU with the skills to succeed in online marketing.

Rating: 4 Stars | **Category:** conference

MozCon - http://moz.com/mozcon

Bringing you the brightest minds in search, social, inbound marketing, and more, MozCon is known for its dynamic, advanced content and idea-filled sessions. Roger, the Mozbot, can't wait to see you. Amazing content from industry leaders. Actionable tips and deep insights. Three days and one amazing experience.

Rating: 4 Stars | **Category:** conference

Black Hat World Conference - http://www.bhwconference.com/

Ready to go to the dark side of SEO? Well, not exactly the dark side, but the gray side mixed with some hype and some secrets and the cognoscenti of technical SEO? Black Hat world is your conference. Learn everything Google doesn't want to tell you amidst some really obnoxious, full-of-themselves smarty pants people from the world of technical SEO. Bring your pleasant smile; you'll need it.

Rating: 4 Stars | **Category:** conference

SearchLove Conference - https://www.distilled.net/events/

SearchLove provides search marketing insight across a 2 day conference. Attendees learn how to drive higher quality traffic to their site, get actionable advice on the latest search engine advancements and discover page conversion strategies, all delivered by search marketing experts who implement these tactics every day.

Rating: 3 Stars | **Category:** conference

PUBCON - http://www.pubcon.com/

Pubcon is an annual social media and optimization conference supported by the industry's leading businesses, speakers, exhibitors, and sponsors involved in social media, Internet marketing, search engines, and digital advertising, and offers an in-depth look at the future of technology presented by the world's top speakers in provocative cutting-edge sessions.

Rating: 3 Stars | **Category:** conference

CONTENT MARKETING WORLD - http://www.contentmarketingworld.com/

Content Marketing World is the one event where you can learn and network with the best and the brightest in the content marketing industry.You will leave with all the materials you need to take a content marketing strategy back to your team – and – to implement a content marketing plan that will grow your business and inspire your audience.

Rating: 3 Stars | **Category:** conference

SEJ SUMMIT 2015 - http://www.searchenginejournal.com/sejsummit2015/

An invite-only, top-shelf conference series for enterprise digital marketers in the US and the UK. Presented by Searchmetrics.

Rating: 2 Stars | **Category:** conference

INBOUND 2016 - http://www.inbound.com/

NBOUND fuels the passion that drives the most innovative and successful business leaders of our time. INBOUND's purpose is to provide the inspiration, education, and connections you need to transform your business. More for content marketing than for SEO, but since content is king...

Rating: 2 Stars | **Category:** conference

CONVERSION CONFERENCE - http://www.conversionconference.com/

Whether you're a web designer, an optimization or analytics pro, a marketer or a business owner, you can learn, grow and profit from the secrets of the highest converting websites in the world by attending Conversion Conference.

Rating: 2 Stars | **Category:** conference

EASTER EGGS

If you're not a computer programmer, you might not know what an "Easter egg" is. "Easter eggs" are hidden, funny secrets hacks inside of computer programs. Since Google is very much an engineering company, it is not surprising that there are secret "Easter eggs" inside the Google search engine.

Here are the best **Easter eggs** on Search Engine Optimization. Check them out and impress your (nerd) friends.

ATARI BREAKOUT - http://google.com/images?q=atari+breakout

Bored at work, and love classic video games? Search Google Images for 'Atari Breakout.' Then use the blue panel at the bottom and your cursor to play (but we didn't have to tell you that, because you remember Atari breakout, right?)

Rating: 5 Stars | **Category:** misc.

DO A BARREL ROLL - http://google.com/search?q=do+a+barrel+roll

Search for 'Do A Barrel Roll' on Google and the screen will, well, roll.

Rating: 5 Stars | **Category:** misc.

ZERG RUSH - http://google.com/search?q=zerg+rush

Zerg rush...that overwhelming attack feeling in a video game. It's also a Google Easter Egg. Type 'zerg rush' into Google and see what happens.

Rating: 5 Stars | **Category:** misc.

ASKEW GOOGLE SEARCH RESULTS - http://google.com/images?q=askew

Light-hearted search results display from Google. Search for 'askew' on Google and it will tilt the results page. Sometimes (but not always) 'tilt' will do the same thing.

Rating: 4 Stars | **Category:** misc.

BLINK HTML - http://google.com/search?q=blink+html

Type 'blink html' into a Google search, and guess what, the words html and blink, will - wait for it - blink.

Rating: 4 Stars | **Category:** misc.

ASK GOOGLE TO DEFINE ANAGRAM - http://google.com/search?q=define:anagram

An anagram, of course, is a word, phrase, or name formed by rearranging the letters of another, such as cinema, to form iceman. If you try to 'define: anagram' on Google, it will ask you if you mean 'nag a ram.' If you try 'define anagram,' it will ask if you mean 'nerd fame again.' Ha, ha. Nerds of the world: unite.

Rating: 4 Stars | **Category:** misc.

GOOGLE GRAVITY - http://mrdoob.com/projects/chromeexperiments/google_gravity

Start at Google, with INSTANT turned off. Type in GOOGLE GRAVITY and click the I'M FEELING LUCKY button. This takes you to mrdoob.com (see URL) where you can have fun with this very interactive vision of Google and Google Gravity.

Rating: 4 Stars | **Category:** misc.

GOOGLE SEARCH FOR FESTIVUS - http://google.com/search?q=festivus

Type 'Festivus' into Google and pay attention to the left side of the page. Festivus, according to Wikipedia, is a parody holiday celebrated on 12/23 as an alternative to commercialized Christmas festivities that dominate the culture.

Rating: 4 Stars | **Category:** misc.

GOOGLE PACMAN - http://google.com/search?q=google+pacman

Type 'Google Pacman' into Google and you can play Pacman. Just click on the famous Google doodle that appears, and use your 'arrow' keys on your keyboard to play. Next, think longingly of that much simpler time before cell phones, YouTube, multilevel multidimensional multiplayer games, and no driving while texting. Ah, it was so good before it all become so wonderful.

Rating: 4 Stars | **Category:** resource

ROLL A DIE - http://google.com/search?q=roll+a+die

Need to roll a die? (You know, what some people call a 'dice,' when really they mean just one, which is a die.) Anyway, just type 'roll a die' into Google and a dice simulator pops up. We mean a 'die' simulator, but not that kind of 'die.' Oh ugh.

Rating: 3 Stars | **Category:** misc.

BLETCHLEY PARK - http://google.com/search?q=bletchley+park

Do a Google search for 'bletchley park,' and watch Google decode the name on the search results page. (Bletchley Park was the place where the British broke the German secret codes during World War II).

Rating: 3 Stars | **Category:** misc.

ANSWER TO THE ULTIMATE QUESTION OF LIFE, THE UNIVERSE, AND EVERYTHING - http://bit.ly/ypqeE9

Search Google for 'answer to the ultimate question of life, the universe, and everything' and it returns the phrase = 42, a reference to The Hitchhiker's Guide to the Galaxy, by Douglas Adams.

Rating: 3 Stars | **Category:** misc.

RECURSION ON GOOGLE - http://google.com/search?q=recursion

Recursion, of course means 'the repeated application of a recursive procedure or definition.' Search Google for either 'recursion' or 'define:recursion' and you'll see 'Did you mean: recursion?'at the top of the search results page. Get it? Nerd humor.

Rating: 3 Stars | **Category:** misc.

USE THE FORCE LUKE - https://youtube.com/results?search_query=use+the+force+luke

Technically this is a YouTube easter egg, but search YouTube for Use the Force Luke', and watch the page move around, randomly...as if it were being moved by the 'Force.' Must be a Star Wars nerd to get this one.

Rating: 3 Stars | **Category:** misc.

THE LONELIEST NUMBER - http://google.com/search?q=the+loneliest+number

Search for 'the loneliest number' and Google returns: 1. As in the song.

Rating: 3 Stars | **Category:** misc.

WEBDRIVER TORSO - http://google.com/search?q=webdriver+torso

Type in 'Webdriver Torso' to Google and the logo on the top left becomes a series of blinking blocks. Click on the link to Wikipedia to learn that: 'Webdriver Torso is a YouTube account made by Google that posts mostly 11-second videos consisting of blue and red rectangles that change position, accompanied by a series of beeps which change in pitch. '

Rating: 3 Stars | **Category:** resource

CONWAY'S GAME OF LIFE - https://google.com/search?q=conway's+game+of+life

Type 'Conway's Game of Life' into Google, and watch the far right of the screen evolve. Then click the first search result from Wikipedia, to learn what 'Conway's Game of Life' is really about.

Rating: 3 Stars | **Category:** tool

GOOGLE IN 1998 - https://google.com/search?q=google+in+1998

Flashback. Party like it's 1999. We mean 1998. Type 'Google in 1998,' and Google will show you what its search results looked like at the very beginning.

Rating: 3 Stars | **Category:** misc.

BEAM ME UP SCOTTY -
https://youtube.com/results?search_query=beam+me+up+scotty

If you like Star Trek, and you like YouTube, you'll like this easter egg. Search YouTube for 'Beam me up Scotty' and the results will be 'beamed over' to you.

Rating: 3 Stars | **Category:** misc.

FLIP A COIN - http://google.com/search?q=flip+a+coin

Need to flip a coin? Who carries real coins these days? Just Google 'Flip a Coin,' and Google will provide you a coin flip simulator. Next up: Bitcoin flips.

Rating: 2 Stars | **Category:** misc.

LET ME GOOGLE THAT FOR YOU - http://lmgtfy.com

Ever really need to 'show' someone how to Google something? This third-party Google 'easter egg' does just that. Worth a chuckle. 1) type a search query, 2) copy / paste the quick link it generates into your browser address bar, or send it to a friend, 3) when you load that link, it will 'literally' walk you through how to Google it.

Rating: 2 Stars | **Category:** misc.

DO THE HARLEM SHAKE -
http://youtube.com/results?search_query=do+the+harlem+shake

Go to YouTube and type in 'Do the Harlem Shake,' and pay attention the YouTube logo on the left. If you have sound, you'll also hear the obnoxious music. Cool, huh?

Rating: 2 Stars | **Category:** misc.

GOOGLE I'M FEELING LUCKY - https://www.google.com/webhp?hl=en

Just go to the primary, empty Google screen. Hold your mouse over the 'I'm Feeling Lucky' button for a few seconds. It will scroll through suggestions such as 'I'm feeling generous'. Funny? Does anyone ever click on the 'I'm feeling lucky buton'? Why?

Rating: 2 Stars | **Category:** resource

BACON NUMBER - http://google.com/search?q=kim+kardashian+bacon+number

How many degrees of separation is someone from Kevin Bacon? The answer is called their 'Bacon Number.' Enter a name of a celebrity followed by 'Bacon Number' in Google search, like 'Kim Kardashian Bacon Number,' and Google will tell you.